JAPANESE
SELF-TAUGHT

MARLBOROUGH'S SELF-TAUGHT SERIES–No. 17 JAPANESE

JAPANESE
SELF-TAUGHT

(THIMM'S SYSTEM, IN ROMAN CHARACTERS)

WITH PHONETIC PRONUNCIATION

CONTAINING
THE SYLLABARY; CLASSIFIED VOCABULARIES AND CONVERSATIONS;
TRAVEL TALK, TRADE AND COMMERCE,
ARMY AND NAVY, RELIGION,
POST-OFFICE AND CORRESPONDENCE; THE NUMERALS;
MONEY, WEIGHTS & MEASURES, &C., &C.

EDITED BY

W. J. S. SHAND

Director, School of Japanese Language and Literature,
Birkbeck Bank Chambers, London.

GYAN

Published by

Gyan Publishing House
5, Ansari Road
Daryaganj, New Delhi-110002
Phone: 011-47034999, 9811692060
E-mail: books@gyanbooks.com

Distribution Network
gyanbooks.com
India, USA, Canada, UK, Australia, France

ISBN : 978-81-212-4437-4 (PB)
First Published, 1907

2nd Impression 2020

Printed at: Gyan Press, Delhi.

Japanese Self-Taught
Edited By: W. J. S. Shand

IMPORTANT NOTICE.

The student should bear in mind that the construction of Japanese sentences is entirely different from that of English, and that consequently, whilst the Japanese sentences in this book express the same meaning as the English, they are in the Japanese form and must not be regarded as a literal translation. (See "Syntax" in JAPANESE GRAMMAR SELF-TAUGHT.")

LETCHWORTH
THE GARDEN CITY PRESS LTD.
PRINTERS

PREFACE.

THE particular aim of this book is to meet the need of those who require to make use of the spoken language without the usual expenditure of time and effort necessary to acquiring the grammar. It therefore supplies the words in common every-day use, classified according to subject, including extensive vocabularies for the Army and Navy, Trade and Commerce, Missionary enterprise, Travel, &c., &c., together with a large number of colloquial phrases and sentences of a practical character, similarly classified. Throughout these sections the pronunciation of the Japanese words is added in accordance with Marlborough's well-known system of phonetics, a system which by its simplicity enables anyone speaking English to read off the words at a glance, although previously unacquainted with the language. The student will of course do well to avail himself as far as possible of the services of a competent instructor in order to perfect his pronunciation, etc.; on the other hand, teachers will find in this book a useful supplement to their oral instruction.

The Publishers have had the valuable assistance, as Editor, of Mr. W. J. S. Shand, who was for twenty-seven years resident in Japan, and has had four years' experience as Director of the School of Japanese Language and Literature in London.

For the native characters—the syllabaries—and the rules of transliteration, the student is referred to "JAPANESE GRAMMAR SELF-TAUGHT" (Marlborough's *Self-Taught* Series, No. 18), of which this volume is the complement, the two works forming a very comprehensive and useful manual of the Japanese language for students, naval and military officers and public servants, commercial men and traders, missionaries, travellers and tourists.

London, 1907.

CONTENTS.

PAGE

The Syllabary and Pronunciation 6
  Peculiarities of the Syllabary 10
  The Tonic Accent... 10

Preliminary Notes 11

Vocabularies.—Pages 13 to 71.
  Animals, Vegetables, etc.:—
    Animals, Birds and Fishes 15
    Fruits, Trees, Flowers and Vegetables 17
    Insects and Reptiles 16
  Army and Navy 46
  Colours 18
  Commerce (Trade and) 38
  Correspondence 45
  Countries and Nations 34
  Furniture (House and) 28
  House and Furniture 28
  Mankind: Relations 21
    Body (The Human) 22
    Cooking and Eating Utensils 25
    Dress and Dressing 26
    Food and Drink 24
    Health 23
    Washing List 27
  Navy (Army and)... 46
  Numbers—Cardinal, Auxiliary, Ordinal, Collective and Fractional ... ... 55 to 58
  Parts of Speech ... ... 58 to 71
    Adjectives 58
    Adverbs, Particles, Conjunctions, Pronouns, etc.... ... 69
    Verbs 63
  Post-office, Telegraph and Telephone 45
  Professions, Trades, etc.... 33
  Religion 30
  Ships and Shipping 37
  Telegraph (Post-office, —, and Telephone) 45
  Telephone (Post-office, Telegraph and) 45

CONTENTS.

	PAGE
Times and Seasons	18
Town and Country	20
Trade and Commerce	38
Travelling	35
World and its Elements, The	13
Land and Water	13
Minerals and Metals	14
CONVERSATIONAL PHRASES AND SENTENCES.—Pages 72 to 106.	
Commercial and Trading	103
Conveyances, Hiring	83
Correspondence	95
Enquiries	79
Expressions and Phrases (Useful and Necessary Idiomatic)	72
Expressions of Emotion	77
Health	94
In Town: Visiting	98
Introductions	97
Money (Changing)	106
Post-office, The	95
Shopping	101
Telegrams	95
Time, The	93
Trading (Commercial and)	103
Travelling.—Pages 81 to 92.	
Arrival	86
Hotel, The	87
Meals	90
By Railway	81
By Road: Hiring Conveyances	83
By Steamboat	85
Useful and Necessary Expressions and Phrases	72
Visiting	98
Weather, The	93
MONEY: Equivalent Values—Japanese, English, American...	107
WEIGHTS AND MEASURES	107
POSTAGE	108

JAPANESE SELF-TAUGHT.

THE SYLLABARY AND PRONUNCIATION.

The Japanese language has no "alphabet" as we understand the word. The characters which may be said to correspond with the English alphabet stand for *syllables*—that is, the vowels and the combinations of the vowels and consonants which are employed in the construction of words.

These characters constitute the Syllabary, which therefore consists of (*a*) Vowel syllabics (syllables), and (*b*) Consonant syllabics.

(*a*) The Vowel syllabics represent the simple vowel sounds, *a, i, u, e, o.*

(*b*) The Consonant syllabics stand for the syllables which consist in each case of a consonant and a vowel joined together, as *ka, ki, ku, ke, ko.*

These syllabics together form what is termed the "Go-jiu-on," i.e., the *Fifty Sounds.* As, however, some of the consonantal sounds have softened forms, and final *n* is separately represented, the number of syllables actually employed is greater.

The following table gives a convenient arrangement of the syllabary, the softened forms being printed in italics. (For the syllabaries in the native character see JAPANESE GRAMMAR SELF-TAUGHT, pages 96, 97.)

THE SYLLABARY.

VOWEL SYLLABLES.

a	i	u	e	o

CONSONANT SYLLABLES.

ka *ga*	ki *gi*	ku *gu*	ke *ge*	ko *go*
sa *za*	shi *ji*	su *zu*	se *ze*	so *zo*
ta *da*	chi *ji*	tsu *dzu*	te *de*	to *do*
na	ni	nu	ne	no
ha *ba* *pa*	hi *bi* *pi*	fu *bu* *pu*	he *be* *pe*	ho *bo* *po*
ma	mi	mu	me	mo
ya	i	yu	ye	yo
ra	ri	ru	re	ro
wa	i	u	ye	wo

By learning the nine consonants *k*, *s*, *t*, *n*, *h*, *m*, *y*, *r*, and *w*, togethe with the five consonantal softenings *g*, *z*, *d*, *b*, and *p*, the Syllabary is readily committed to memory.

PRONUNCIATION.

THE VOWELS.

Characters.	Pronunciation.	Phonetic signs.
ā	approximately as *a* in *father*	*ah*
a	„ *a* „ *father*, but shorter	ah
ī (*or* ii)	„ *i* „ *machine*	*ee*
i	„ *i* „ *machine*, but shorter ...	ee

In some words *y* is substituted for *i*, and in a few others *i* is pronounced like *yi* (yee).

ĭ	is almost silent; merely a suspicion of a vowel sound is noticeable	', (ee)
ū	approximately as *oo* in *food*	*oo*
u	„ *oo* „ *foot*	oo
ŭ	like ĭ is almost silent	',(oo)
ē	approximately as *a* „ *date*	*eh*
e	„ *e* „ *bed*	e, eh
ō	„ *o* „ *sore*	*oh*
o	„ *o* „ *polo*	oh

[For remarks on the long and short vowels, see *Preliminary Notes*, pars. 1-2, pp. 11-12.]

THE CONSONANTS.

D, d — is merely the *softened* form of *t*, and is pronounced in a similar manner ... ... d

F, f — In pronouncing *f*, the lower lip does not quite come in contact with the upper teeth, but remains at about the same distance from them as in pronouncing *wh* in the word *when* ... ... f

G, g — at the beginning of a word, hard—like *g* in the English *go*... ... ... g, gh

In all other positions like *ng* in *sing* ... ... ng

H, h — aspirated as in English ... ... h

In *hĭtotsŭ*, hĭ is pronounced like *shĭ*.

R, r — In the syllabic *ri* pronounced somewhat like the English *d*; i.e., in its articulation the tip of the tongue touches the roof of the mouth at the same point as in pronouncing *r*, but substituting the *d* sound ... ... r

In the other syllabics *r* more resembles the English *r*, but in none of them is the trill so decided as in, say, Scotch, French, or German ... ... r

S, s — always sibilant, as in *so*, *sat* ... ... s

T, t — as in Italian; that is, the tip of the tongue is brought into contact with the upper teeth, instead of touching the front part of the roof of the mouth t

Y, y — In the syllable *ye* the *y* is mute in most words, and is sometimes omitted in the Roman character; otherwise as in English ... ... y

In some words *y* is used as a vowel in place of *i* ee

Z, z — like a soft *dz* in *su-zu* and *tsu-zu* ... ... dz

In the syllabics *za*, *ze*, *zo*, as in English ... ... z

The consonants *l*, *q*, *v*, and *x* are entirely absent from the Japanese syllabary. Even an educated Japanese, in speaking English, is apt to substitute *r* for *l*; *q* and *x* are of course unnecessary in the presence of *k* and *s*; and the nearest approach in Japanese to the English *v* is probably *fu*.

C occurs only united with *h*, in the syllable *chi*; *f* only in *fu*; *j* only in the syllable *ji*, which takes the place of *zi* and *di*; and *w* occurs only in *wa* and *wo*. After *k* or *g*, *w* is not sounded except as a provincialism.

The remaining consonants *b*, *k*, *m*, *n*, *p*, have approximately the same sounds as in English, and are therefore allowed to represent their own sounds respectively.

Vowel Combinations.

In the vowel combinations each letter is separately and distinctly sounded; thus,

ai = a + i, and is pronounced "ah'ee," like the English *I*, or *y* in *thy* ... ... *i*, ah'ee

au = a + u, pronounced "ah'oo" or "ow," like *ow* in *now* ow

ae = a + e, „ "ah'eh" ... ... ah'eh

ao = a + o, „ "ah'oh" ... ... ah'oh

ui = u + i, „ "oo'ee" ... ... oo'ee

ei = e + i, „ "eh'ee," like *ay* in *day*, or *ai* in *wait* ... ... ay

oi = o + i, pronounced "oh'ee," like *oy* in *joy*, or *oi* in *boil* ... ... oy

PECULIARITIES OF THE SYLLABARY.
THE TONIC ACCENT.

THE SYLLABARY.—A reference to the Syllabary on page 7, or better still to the Syllabaries in the native characters,* discloses three peculiarities, viz.,

(1) The consonant syllables are composed in each case of a consonant and vowel sound combined—consonant first and vowel following—for every syllable is supposed to end with a vowel and usually does so; as in *nani* (nah'nee), *kata* (kah'tah), *donata* (doh-nah'tah), *gozarimasŭ*† (goh-zah-ree-mah's'). The principal exceptions are foreign words, contractions, and words ending in *n*, as *ban*, *ken*, etc.

(2) There are certain variations from the regular consonants; e.g., *shi* is found instead of *si*, *chi* instead of *ti*, *fu* instead of *hu*, &c, This is owing to the fact that the Japanese are unable to pronounce the sounds which are displaced.

(3) The consonants k, s, t, and h have *softened* forms. These are to be regarded merely as modifications of the hard consonants, and not as different ones. The modification is indicated in the native character by adding a diacritic sign to the hard consonant symbol; thus, *ko* accompanied by the sign is read *go*, *tsu* with the sign is read *dzu*, &c.

ACCENT.—The accentuation of Japanese words is much less prominent than that of English. Quickened, or silenced, vowel sounds frequently render prominent the other portions of the word, but, as a general rule, the stress is laid about equally on each syllable. The sound of the word *gozarimasŭ*, for example, is almost evenly emphasized—*go-za-ri-ma-sŭ* (goh-zah-ree-mah's'), the terminal *u* being nearly inaudible, and the syllable *ma* receiving but a very slight accent, the emphasis over and above the stress laid on the other three syllables being barely perceptible.

(*a*) In words of *two syllables* the accent is, as a rule, on the *first* syllable, as *hiro* (hee'roh), *tsuru* (tsoo'roo).

EXCEPTIONS.—When the vowel sound of the first syllable is short *i* or *a*, *shĭka* (sh'kah'), *tsŭki* (ts'kee'), *hirō* (hee-roh'), *musŭ* (moo-soo').

* *Japanese Grammar Self-Taught*, pp. 96, 97. † In Tokyo, *gozaimasŭ*.

(*b*) In words of *three syllables* the accent is, as a rule, on the *second* syllable, as *arashi* (ah-rah'shee), *motomŭ* (moh-toh'm').

Exception.—When the second syllable is short, as ĭ or ŭ, the first syllable bears the accent, unless the final syllable has a double (long) vowel sound; in which case the primary accent is laid on the last syllable, and a second (subordinate) accent on the first, as *taĭra* [tah'(ee)rah], *atsŭku* (ah'ts'koo); *chikŭshō* (chee-k'-shoh'), *bokŭtō* (boh-k'toh').

(*c*) In *polysyllables* the accent is on the *last syllable but one*, as *Hakodate* (hah-koh-dah'teh), *Yokohama* (yoh-koh-hah'mah).

Exception.—If the last syllable but one contains ĭ or ŭ, the accent is thrown back upon the preceding syllable, as *Shimotsŭke* (shee-moh'ts'keh).

In *all* words accent goes to long syllables, and whenever two such long syllables come together they are pronounced with equal stress. Examples: *Aimashō* (*i*-mah-sh*oh*'), *hōbō* (h*oh*-b*oh*), *shōsō* (sh*oh*-s*oh*).

PRELIMINARY NOTES.

In order to make the best progress in acquiring the words and sentences in the following pages, the student is recommended to learn a few at a time by repeating them aloud with the aid of the phonetic pronunciation in the third column. Those who have studied Japanese Grammar Self-Taught (No. 18 of this series) will find the conversational phrases and sentences very useful matter for exercise in writing as well as in speaking Japanese.

Pronunciation.—Although the system of phonetics may seem a little cumbersome at first, practice will soon enable the student to pronounce the words easily and naturally. The following hints may be of service:—

(1) The pronunciation, as explained on pp. 8-11, should be carefully studied, and the fact particularly noted that the Japanese vowels always have the same *quality* or kind of sound, although they vary in length; they are not used to represent

quite different sounds like the English vowels (as for example the vowel *a* in the words *mar, make, man, many, woman*); they should be pronounced very *short*, i.e., they should not be dwelt upon, except where specially marked long (*ā, ī, ū, ē, ō*), and when double, *aa, ii, uu*.

Note that in the phonetic columns in the following pages attention is drawn to the *long* and *double* vowels by printing their phonetic equivalents in *Italics*, thus: *ah, ee, oo, eh, oh.*

(2) The very short vowels *ĭ* and *ŭ* have little more effect than that of causing the preceding consonant to be held out to enable the following one to be joined on to it; thus, *shĭki* (sh'kee).

These almost inaudible vowels are represented, it will be noticed, either by an apostrophe merely, or by the phonetic sign in brackets, according to convenience; e.g., *tetsŭ* (teh'ts'), *uma* [(oo)m-mah'].

In other cases where alternative phonetic signs are employed, their respective uses depend on the question as to which will the better conduce to correct pronunciation.

(3) Bear in mind that *i* (italic) always represents the diphthong ah-ee—i.e., the sound of "i" in *line, tile*, etc., or the pronoun "I."

(4) Each *syllable* in Japanese should be distinctly sounded, so that where two consonants meet (except in *ch, ts*, and *dz*) they must be pronounced separately; thus, *onna* = ohn'nah, *katta* = kaht'tah.

(5) The tonic accent should be very slight, and allowed to fall naturally. Its incidence is shown by a dash ('), as in *kiri* (kee'ree); where no syllable is thus marked the stress is evenly distributed.

(6) The student should omit no opportunity of correcting and perfecting his pronunciation by hearing the language spoken by a native of *Tokyo* by preference, or by a foreign expert.

Those who desire to become acquainted with the language in its own character, as an introduction to Japanese literature, will find the native syllabaries, together with the rules of transliteration and illustrative examples, in JAPANESE GRAMMAR SELF-TAUGHT, pp. 96-102.

VOCABULARIES.*

1. The World and its Elements.

(Chikyu to sono genso.)

English.	Japanese (romanized).	Pronunciation.
Air	*kūki*	koo'kee
cloud	*kumo*	koo'moh
cold	*samusa*	sah-moo'sah
darkness	*kura-gari*	koo'rah-ngah'ree
earth	*tsŭchi*	ts(oo)chee'
East	*higashi*	hee-ngah'shee
fire	*hi*	hee
fog	*kiri*	kee'ree
frost	*shimo*	shee'moh
hail	*arare*	ah-rah'reh
heat	*danki*	dahn'kee
light	*hikari*	heekah'ree
lightning	*inabikari*	eenahbeekah'ree
moon	*tsuki*	tsoo'kee
North	*kita*	kee'tah
rainbow	*niji*	nee'jee
shade	*kage*	kah'ngeh
sky	*sora*	soh'rah
South	*minami*	meenah'mee
stars	*hoshi*	hoh'shee
storm	*arashi*	ahrah'shee
sun	*hi, taiyō*	hee, *ti*-yoh'
thaw	*yuki-doke*	yoo'kee-doh'keh
thunder	*kaminari*	kahmeenah'ree
weather	*yōki, tenki*	yoh'kee, ten'kee
West	*nishi*	nee'shee
wind	*kaze*	kah'zeh

2. Land and Water. *(Oka to mizu.)*

English.	Japanese (romanized).	Pronunciation.
Bay	*wan*	wahn
beach	*umibe, hamabe*	oomee'beh, hahmah'beh
cliff	*gake*	gah'keh
coast, shore	*kaigan, ura*	ki'ngahn, oo'rah

* For notes on ARTICLES, GENDER, &c., see *Japanese Grammar Self-Taught* (Marlborough's Self-Taught Series, No. 18), pp. 16 and 17.

English.	Japanese (romanized).	Pronunciation.
ice	*kōri*	k*oh'* ree
island	*shima*	shee'mah
lake	*kosui*	kohsoo'ee
land	*tochi, oka*	toh'chee, oh'kah
mud	*doro*	doh'roh
rain	*ame*	ah'meh
river	*kawa*	kah'wah
rock	*iwa*	ee'wah
sea	*umi*	oo'mee
snow	*yuki*	yoo'kee
stream	*nagare, ko-gawa*	nah-ngah'reh, koh-ngah'-[wah
tide	*shiwo*	shee'woh
water	*mizu*	meedz'
waterfall	*taki*	tah'kee
wave	*nami*	nah'mee
world	*sekai*	seh-k*i'*

3. Minerals and Metals. (*Kwō-butsu to kinzoku.*)

Brass	*shinchū*	sheench*oo'*
bronze	*kara-kane*	kah'rah-kah'neh
cement	*semento*	seh-men'toh
clay	*hena-tsŭchi*	heh-nah-ts'chee
coal	*sekitan*	seh'keetahn
concrete	*konkurito*	kon-koo-ree-toh
copper	*akagane*	ahkah-ngah'neh
diamond	*kongōseki*	koh-ng*oh*-seh-kee
emerald	*emerado*	eh-meh-rah'doh
glass	*gyaman*	ghee-ah'mahn
gold	*kin*	keen
granite	*mikage-ishi*	meekah'ngeh-ee'shee
iron	*tetsŭ*	teh'ts'
—, cast	*nabe-gane*	nah'beh-ngah'neh
—, wrought	*juku tetsŭ*	joo'koo teh'ts'
lead	*namari*	nahmah'ree
lime	*ishibai*	eesheeb*i'*
marble	*rōseki*	r*oh'*seh-kee
mercury	*sui-gin*	soo'ee-ngheen
pearl	*shinju*	sheen'joo
silver	*gin*	gheen
slate	*sekiban*	seh-kee'bahn

English.	Japanese (romanized).	Pronunciation.
steel	*hagane*	hah-ngah'neh
stone	*ishi*	ee'shee
tin	*suzu*	soo'dzoo
zinc	*totan*	toh'tahn

4. Animals, Birds, and Fishes. (*Dōbutsū, tori, sakana.*)

English.	Japanese (romanized).	Pronunciation.
Animal	*kemono*	keh-moh'noh
barking	*hoeru*	hoh-eh'roo
bear	*kuma*	koo'mah
bird	*tori*	toh'ree
blackbird	*hiyodori*	hee-yoh-doh'ree
bull	*o-ushi*	oh-oo'shee
calf	*ko-ushi*	koh-oo'shee
cat	*neko*	neh'koh
cattle	*ushi-rui*	oo' shee-roo'ee
chicken	*hiyokko*	hee-yohk'koh
cock	*on-dori*	ohn-doh'ree
cod	*tara*	tah'rah
cow	*me-ushi*	meh-oo'shee
crab	*kani*	kah'nee
dog	*inu*	ee'noo
donkey	*roba*	roh'bah
duck	*ahiru*	ah-hee'roo
eagle	*washi*	wah'shee
eel	*unagi*	oonah'nghee
fish	*sakana, uwo*	sah-kah'nah, oo'woh
fox	*kitsune*	keetsoo'neh
goat	*hitsuji*	heetsoo'jee
goose	*yachō*	gah-ch*oh'*
grouse	*yezo-raichō*	yeh'zoh-ri-ch*oh'*
hair	*ke*	keh
hen	*mendori*	men-doh'ree
herd	*ushi*	oo'shee
herring	*nishin*	nee'sheen
hoof	*hizume, tsume*	heedzoo'meh, tsoo'meh
horse	*ŭma*	'm-mah'
lamb	*kohitsuji*	koh-hee-tsoo'jee
lark (Jap.)	*hibari*	hee-bah'ree
lion	*shishi*	shee'shee
lobster	*kuruma-ebi*	kooroo'mah-eh'bee

English.	Japanese (romanized).	Pronunciation.
monkey	*saru*	sah'roo
mouse	*hatsŭka-nezumi*	hah'ts'kah-neh-dzoo'mee
mule	*usagi-ŭma*	oo-sah'nghee-'m-mah'
owl	*fukurō*	fookooro*h*'
ox	*kinkiri-ushi*	keen-kee'ree-oo'shee
oysters	*kaki*	kah'kee
parrot	*ōmu*	*oh*'moo
partridge	*shako*	shah'koh
pheasant	*kiji*	kee'jee
pig	*buta*	boo'tah
pike (sea-)	*kamasu*	kahmah'soo
rat	*nezumi*	neh-dzoo'mee
salmon	*shake*	shah'keh
sea-fish	*umi-uwo*	oo'mee-oo'woh
seal	*azarashi*	ah-zahrah'shee
sheep	*hitsuji*	hee-tsoo'jee
snipe	*shigi*	shee'nghee
sole	*shĭta-birame*	sh'tah-bee-rah'meh
sparrow (tree-)	*suzume*	soodzoo'meh
swallow	*tsubakuro, tsubame*	tsoobahkoo'roh,tsoobah'-
swan	*hakuchō*	hah-koo-ch*oh*' [meh
tiger	*tora*	toh'rah
trout	*yamame*	yahmah'meh
turbot	*ishigarei*	eeshee-ngah-ray'
turkey	*shĭchi-men-chō*	sh'chee-men-ch*oh*
turtle	*shōgakubō*	sh*oh*-ngah-koob*oh*
whale	*kujira*	koo-jee'rah

5. Insects and Reptiles. (*Mushi; ha-ko-dōbutsu.*)

English.	Japanese (romanized).	Pronunciation.
Ant	*ari*	ah'ree
bee	*hachi*	hah'chee
beetle	*tama-mushi, kabutō-*	tah'mah- (*or* kahbooto*h*-)
butterfly	*chōchō* [*mushi*	ch*oh*-ch*oh* [moo'shee
caterpillar	*kemushi, sanagi*	keh-moo'shee, sah-nah'
fly	*hai*	hi [nghee
frog	*kaeru*	kah'eh-roo
gnat	*buyu*	boo'yoo
insect	*mushi*	moo'shee
lizard	*tokage*	tohkah'ngeh
mosquito	*ka*	kah

English.	Japanese (romanized).	Pronunciation.
silkworm	*kaiko*	k*i*'koh
snail	*dede mushi*	deh-deh-moo'shee
snake	*hebi*	heh'bee
spider	*kumo*	koo'moh

6. Trees, Fruits, Flowers, and Vegetables.

(*Mizu-gewashi; kudamono; hana; ao-mono yasai.*)

(See Shopping, p. 101.)

English.	Japanese (romanized).	Pronunciation.
Apple	*ringo*	reen'-ngoh
apricot	*anzu*	ahn'dzoo
ash	*toneriko*	tohnehree'koh
asparagus	*ūdo*	*oo*'doh
beans	*mame*	mah'meh
beech-tree	*buna*	boo'nah
beetroot	*aka-daikon*	ah'kah-d*i*'kohn
birch	*kaba-no-ki*	kah'bah-noh-kee
cabbage	*kabeji*	kah-beh-jee
carrot	*ninjin*	neen'jeen
cauliflower	*hana-kabeji*	hah'nah-kah-beh-jee
celery	*sereri*	seh-reh-ree
cherry (eating)	*sakurambo*	sahkoorahm'boh
cucumber	*kyūri*	kee-*oo*'ree
figs	*ichijiku*	eecheejee'koo
fir-tree	*momi*	moh'mee
grapes	*budō*	bood*oh*'
leaf	*ha*	hah
lemon	*yuzu*	yoo'dzoo
lettuce	*retasu*	reh-tah's'
lily	*yuri*	yoo'ree
lime	*raimu*	r*i*'-moo
melon	*uri, makuwa-uri*	oo'ree, mah-koo'wah-oo'-ree
nut	*mi*	mee
oak-tree	*kashi*	kah'shee
peach	*momo*	moh'moh
pear	*nashi*	nah'shee
peas (green)	*endo-mame*	en'doh-mah'meh
pine (tree)	*matsŭ-no-ki*	mah'ts'-noh-kee
pineapple	*ananasŭ*	ah-nah-nah-s'
plum	*sumomo*	soomoh'moh
potatoes	*jaga-imo*	jah'ngah-ee'moh

English	Japanese (romanized).	Pronunciation.
rose	*bara*	bah'rah
spinach	*hōrensō*	ho*h*renso*h*
strawberry	*oranda-ichigo*	ohrahn'dah-eechee'ngoh
tomato	*aka-nasu*	ah'kah-nah'soo
tree, wood	*ki*	kee
tulip	*ukkonko*	ook-kohn'koh
turnip	*kabu*	kah'boo
vine (grape)	*budō-zuru*	boodo*h*'-dzoo'roo
violet	*sumiresō*	soo-mee-reh-so*h*'
walnut	*kurumi*	kooroo'mee

7. Colours. (*Iro.*)

Black	*kuroi*	kooroy'
blue	*asagi-iro*	ah-sah'nghee-ee'roh
brown	*tobi-iro*	toh'bee-ee'roh
crimson	*shō-jō-hi*	sho*h*-jo*h*-hee
dark	*koi*	koy
green	*aoi, midori-iro*	ah-oy, meedoh'ree-ee'roh
grey	*nedzumi-iro*	neh-dzoo'mee-ee'roh
light (pale)	*usui*	oo-soo'ee
pink	*toki-iro*	toh'kee-ee'roh
purple	*murasaki-iro*	moorahsah'kee-ee'roh
red	*akai, aka-iro*	ah-ki, ahkah-ee'roh
scarlet	*hi-iro*	hee-ee'roh
violet	*kikyō-iro*	kee-k(ee)yo*h*'-ee'roh
white	*shiroi, shiro-iro*	shee-roy, shee'roh-ee'roh
yellow	*ki-iro, kii roi*	kee-ee'roh, kee-roy'

8. Times and Seasons. (*Jikoku, Jisetsu.*)

(For Conversations see page 93.)

Afternoon	*hiru-sugi*	hee'roo-soo'nghee
Christmas	*kurisumasu*	koo-ree-soo-mah-soo
dawn	*ake-gata*	ah'keh-ngah'tah
day	*hi*	hee
days of the week	*shū-kan no hi*	sh*oo*-kahn hoh hee
Sunday	*nichiyōbi*	nee'chee-yo*h*'bee
Monday	*getsuyōbi*	geh-tsoo-yo*h*'bee
Tuesday	*kwayōbi*	k(w)ah-yo*h*'bee
Wednesday	*suiyōbi*	soo-ee-yo*h*'bee
Thursday	*mokuyōbi*	moh-koo-yo*h*'bee

English.	Japanese (romanized).	Pronunciation.
Friday	*kin-yōbi*	keen-y*oh*'bee
Saturday	*doyōbi*	doh-*yoh*'bee
day-time	*hiru*	hee'roo
Easter	*iisuta*	*ee*'soo-tah
evening	*yūgata, ban*	*yoo*'ngah-tah, bahn
every day	*mainichi*	m*i*-nee'chee
fortnight	*ni-shū-kan*	nee-sh*oo*-kahn
Good-Friday	*gū-furaide*	*goo*-foo-r*i*'deh
holiday	*sai-jitsu*	s*i*-jee'tsoo
hour	*ichi-jikan*	ee-chee-jee'kahn
—, half-an-	*han-jikan*	hahn-jee'kahn
mid day, noon	*hiru*	hee'roo
midnight	*yonaka*	yoh-nah'kah
minute	*ip-pun*	eep-poon
month	*hĭto-tsuki*	sh'toh-tsoo'kee
months (the)	*tsuki*	tsoo'kee
January	*shō-gwatsu*	sh*oh*-ng(w)ah'tsoo
February	*ni-gwatsu*	nee-ng(w)ah'tsoo
March	*san-gwatsu*	sahn-ng(w)ah'tsoo
April	*shi-gwatsu*	shee-ng(w)ah'tsoo
May	*go-gwatsu*	goh-ng(w)ah'tsoo
June	*roku-gwatsu*	roh'koo-ng(w)ah' tsoo
July	*shĭchi-gwatsu*	sh(ee)chee'ng(w)ah'tsoo
August	*hachi-gwatsu*	hah'chee-ng(w)ah'tsoo
September	*ku-gwatsu*	koo-ng(w)ah'tsoo
October	*jū-gwatsu*	j*oo*-ng(w)ah'tsoo
November	*jū-ichi-gwatsu*	j*oo*-ee'chee-ng(w)ah'tsoo
December	*jū ni-gwatsu*	j*oo* nee-ng(w)ah'tsoo
morning	*asa*	ah'sah
night	*ban, yoru*	bahn, yoh'roo
quarter (3 months)	*sanga-getsu*	sahn'ngah-geh'tsoo
seasons, the four	*shi-ki*	shee-kee
Spring	*haru*	hah'roo
Summer	*natsŭ*	nah'ts'
Autumn	*aki*	ah'kee
Winter	*fuyu*	foo'yoo
second	*kata-toki*	kah'tah-toh'kee
sunrise	*hi-no-de*	hee-noh-deh
sunset	*hi-no-iri*	hee-noh-ee'ree
time	*toki*	toh'kee

English.	Japanese (romanized).	Pronunciation.
to-day	*konnichi, kyō**	kohn-nee'chee, kee-*oh'*
to-morrow	*myonichi, ashĭta**	mee-oh-nee'chee, ah'-sh'tah
— morning	*ashĭta no asa*	ahsh'tah noh ah'sah
to-night	*komban, kon-ya*	kohm'bahn, kohn-yah
twilight	*kure-gata*	koo'reh-ngah'tah
week	*isshūkan*	ees-sh*oo*'kahn
year	*toshi*	toh'shee
yearly	*mai-nen*	m*i*-nen
yesterday	*kinō, sakujitsu*†	keen*oh'*, sah-koo-jee'tsoo

9. Town and Country. (*Machi to inaka.*)

(For Conversations see page 93.)

Bridge	*hashi*	hah'shee
building (edifice)	*tatemono*	tahteh-moh'noh
bush	*kusamura*	koosah-moo'rah
country	*inaka*	eenah'kah
ditch	*hori, dobu*	hoh'ree, doh'boo
farm	*hata, denji*	hah'tah, den'jee
fence	*kaki*	kah'kee
field	*hatake*	hahtah'keh
foot-path	*ko-michi*	koh-mee'chee
forest	*mori*	moh'ree
gate	*mon*	mohn
grass	*shiba*	shee'bah
hay	*magusa*	mah-ngoo'sah
hut	*koya*	koh'yah
inn	*hatago ya, yadoya*	hah-tah'ngoh-yah, yah-doh'yah
lane	*hoso-michi*	hoh'soh-mee'chee
market	*ichi*	ee'chee
meadow	*maki-ba*	mah'kee-bah
mile	*ichi-mairu*	ee'chee-m*i*'roo
mill-wheel	*mizu-guruma*	mee'dzoo-ngooroo'mah
monument	*kinen-pi*	kee'nen-pee
palace	*kyūjō, goten*	kee-*oo*j*oh*, goh'ten
police-station	*keisatsŭ-jo*	kaysah'ts'-joh
prison	*kangoku*	kahn-ngoh'koo
river	*kawa*	kah'wah
road	*michi*	mee'chee

* Less polite. † More polite.

English.	Japanese (romanized).	Pronunciation.
school	*gakkō*	gahk-k*oh'*
shepherd	*hitsuji-kai*	hee-tsoo'jee-k*i*
shop	*mise*	mee'seh
street	*tōri, machi*	toh'ree, mah'chee
town	*tokai, machi*	toh-k*i'*, mah'chee
valley	*tani*	tah'nee
village	*mura*	moo'rah
well, a	*ido*	ee'doh
wood, a	*mori*	moh'ree

10. Mankind: Relations. (*Ningen: Shinrui.*)

Aunt	*oba*	oh'bah
boy	*musŭko*	moo's'koh
brother	*kyō-dai*	kee-*oh'*-d*i*
brother-in-law	*ko-jū-to*	koh-j*oo*-toh
child	*ko, kodomo*	koh, koh-doh'moh
cousin	*itoko*	ee-toh'koh
daughter	*musŭme*	moo's'meh
daughter-in-law	*uchi no yome*	oo'chee noh yoh'meh
family	*iye*	ee'yeh
father	*chichi*	chee'chee
father-in-law	*shūto*	sh*oo'*toh
girl	*musŭme*	moo's'meh
granddaughter	*mago-musŭme*	mah'ngoh-moo's'meh
grandfather	*ojii-san*	oh-j*ee'*sahn
grandmother	*obā-san*	oh-b*ah'*sahn
grandson	*mago*	mah'ngoh
husband	*otto*	oht'toh
man	*otoko*	oh-toh'koh
marriage	*kekkon*	kek'kohn
mother	*ha-ha*	hah-hah
mother-in-law	*shūto-me*	sh*oo'*toh-meh
nephew	*oi*	oy
niece	*me*	meh
parents	*oya, ryō-shin*	oh'yah, ry*oh'*-sheen
relations	*shinrui*	sheen-roo'ee
sister (elder)	*ane*	ah'neh
— (younger)	*imōto*	ee-m*oh'*toh
sister-in-law	*kojyūtome*	koh-jee-*oo'*toh-meh
son	*musuko*	moo's'koh

English.	Japanese (romanized).	Pronunciation.
son-in-law	*muko*	moo'koh
uncle	*oji*	oh'jee
widow	*goke*	goh'keh
widower	*yamome*	yah-moh'meh
wife	*nyōbo*	nee-*oh*'boh
woman	*onna*	ohn'nah

11. The Human Body. (*Jintai; karada.*)

(See Conversations on Health, page 91.)

Ankle	*ashi-kubi*	ah'shee-koo'bee
arm	*ude*	oo'deh
back	*senaka*	seh-nah'kah
beard	*hige*	hee'ngeh
body	*karada*	kahrah'dah
bones	*hone*	hoh'neh
bowels	*harawata*	hahrahwah'tah
brain	*nō*	no*h*
breast, chest	*mune*	moo'neh
chin	*ago*	ah'ngoh
ear (external)	*mimi*	mee'mee
elbow	*hiji*	hee'jee
eye	*me*	meh
face	*kao*	kah'oh
fingers	*yubi*	yoo'bee
foot	*ashi*	ah'shee
hair	*atama-no-ke*	ah-tah'mah-noh-keh
hand	*te*	teh
head	*atama*	ah-tah'mah
heart	*shin-no-zo*	sheen-noh-zoh
knee	*hiza*	hee'zah
leg	*ashi*	ah'shee
limbs	*te-ashi*	teh-ah'shee
lips	*kuchi-biru*	koo'chee-bee'roo
liver	*kimo, kan-no-zō*	kee'moh, kahn-noh-zo*h*
lungs	*hai-no-zō*	hi-noh-zo*h*
moustache	*uwa hige*	oo'wah hee'ngeh
mouth	*kuchi*	koo'chee
neck	*kubi*	koo'bee
nose	*hana*	hah'nah
shoulders	*kata*	kah'tah

English.	Japanese (romanized).	Pronunciation.
side	*waki*	wah'kee
skin	*kawa*	kah'wah
stomach	*i, i-bukuro*	ee, ee-bookoo'roh
teeth	*ha*	hah
throat	*nodo*	noh'doh
thumb	*oya-yubi*	oh'yah-yoo'bee
toe	*ashi-no-yubi*	ah'shee-no-yoo'bee
tongue	*shĭta*	sh(ee)tah'
wrist	*te-kubi*	teh-koo'bee

12. Health. (*Karada no ambai.*)

(For Conversations see page 94.)

Ambulance	*kega-nin guruma*	keh-ngah-neen goo-roo'-mah
bandage	*hōtai*	ho*h*'ti
bite	*kami-kizu*	kah'mee-kee'dzoo
blind person (a)	*mekura*	meh-koo'rah
bruise	*uchi-mi*	oo'chee-mee
burn	*yakedo*	yahkeh'doh
chemist	*yakuten*	yah-koo'ten
chill	*samuke*	sahmoo'keh
—, to catch a	*kaze wo hiku*	kah'zeh woh hee'koo
contagion	*densen*	den'sen
corns	*kutsŭ-mame*	koo'ts'-mah'meh
cough	*seki*	seh'kee
cure, to	*naosu*	nah'oh-s'
dentist	*ha-isha*	hah-ee'shah
diarrhœa	*kudashi, geri*	koo-dah'shee, gheh'ree
disease, illness	*byō-ki, yamai*	bee-*oh*'kee, yah-mi'
doctor	*isha*	ee'shah
doctor's fee	*yakurei*	yahkooray'
faint, to	*kizetsŭ suru*	kee-zeh'ts' soo'roo
fever	*netsŭ*	neh'ts'
fracture	*dankotsŭ*	dahn-koh'ts'
gout	*tsŭ-fŭ*	tsoo-foo
headache	*dzu-tsŭ*	dzoo-tsoo
hospital	*byōin*	bee-*oh*'een
ill, sick	*fu-kwai, byō-ki*	foo-k(w)*i*, bee-*oh*-kee
indigestion (temporary)	*shoku-atari*	shoh'koo-ah-tah'ree
— (chronic)	*i-byō*	ee-bee-*oh*'
inflammation	*kinshō*	keen-sh*oh*'

English.	Japanese (romanized).	Pronunciation.
medicine	*kusuri*	koosoo'ree
ointment	*kō-yaku*	ko*h*-yah'koo
pain	*itami*	eetah'mee
pill	*gwanyaku*	gwahn-yah'koo
poison	*doku-yaku*	doh'koo-yah'koo
poultice	*pappu*	pahp'poo
prescription	*shohō-yaki*	shoh-ho*h'*-ngah'kee
scald	*yakedo*	yahkeh'doh
sea-sickness	*funa-yoi*	foo'nah-yoy
sore throat	*nodo kataru*	noh-doh kahtah'roo
sprain	*kujiki*	koojee'kee
tonic	*kyōsō-zai, oginai-gusuri*	kee-o*h*-so*h*-zi, oh-nghee-ni'ngoo-soo'ree
wound	*kega*	keh'ngah

13. Food and Drink. (*Shokumotsu to nomi mono.*)

(See also pages 15 to 18. For Conversations see pages 90—92.)

English.	Japanese (romanized).	Pronunciation.
Bacon	*shiwo-buta, beikon*	shee'wo-bootah,bay'kohn
beef	*ushi, gyū-niku*	oo'shee, ghee-*oo'*-nee'koo
beef-steak	*bifu-teki*	bee'foo-teh'kee
beer, ale	*biiru*	b*ee'*roo
bottle	*tokkuri*	tohk-koo'ree
bread	*pan*	pahn
—, brown	*kuro-pan*	koo'roh-pahn
breakfast	*asa-han*	ah'sah-hahn
butter	*bata*	bah'tah
cake	*kwashi*	k(w)ah'shee
cheese	*chiisu*	ch*ee'*soo
chocolate	*chokoretsŭ*	chohkohreh'ts'
cigar	*shigaru*	shee-ngah'roo
coffee	*kōhii*	ko*h'*h*ee*
cream	*kuriimu*	koor*ee'*moo
dinner	*ya-shoku*	yah-shoh'koo
eggs	*tamago*	tah-mah'ngoh
fat (meat)	*shiromi*	sheeroh'mee
flour	*udonko*	oodohn'koh
ham	*hamu*	hah'moo
jam	*jami*	jah'mee
lamb	*ko-hitsuji*	koh-hee-tsoo'jee
lean	*akami*	ah-kah'mee

English.	Japanese (romanized).	Pronunciation.
lemonade	*ramune*	rahmoo'neh
meat	*niku*	nee'koo
milk	*ushi no chichi*	oo'shee noh chee'chee
mustard	*karashi*	kahrah'shee
mutton	*maten, hitsuji no [niku*	mah'ten, hee-tsoo'jee noh [nee'koo
oil	*abura*	ahboo'rah
onion	*negi*	neh'nghee
pepper	*koshō*	koh-sh*oh'*
pork	*buta no niku*	boo'tah noh nee'koo
pudding	*purin*	poo'reen
rice (plant)	*ine*	ee'neh
— (grain)	*kome*	koh'meh
— (boiled)	*meshi*	meh'shee
salad	*sarado*	sahrah'doh
salt	*shiwo*	shee'woh
sausage	*sashidzu*	sah-shee'dzoo
soda-water	*sōda-midzŭ*	s*oh'*dah-mee'dz'
soup	*soppu*	sohp'poo
sugar	*satō*	sahto*h'*
supper	*yūmeshi, yuhan*	y*oo'*meh-shee, yoo-hahn
tea	*cha*	chah
tobacco	*tabako*	tahbah'koh
veal	*ko-ushi no niku*	koh-oo'shee noh nee'koo
vegetables	*yasai-mono*	yahs*i'*-moh'noh
vinegar	*su*	soo
water (drinking)	*nomi-midzŭ*	noh'mee-mee'dz'
wine	*budōshu*	bood*oh'*shoo

14. Cooking and Eating Utensils. (*Ryōri to dōgu.*)

(For Shopping see page 101.)

Basin (slop-)	*koboshi*	kohboh'shee
coffee-pot	*kōhii yakan*	ko*h'hee* yah'kahn
cruet-stand	*yakumi-tate*	yahkoo'mee-tah'teh
cup	*wan*	wahn
dish	*naga-sara*	nah'ngah-sah'rah
fork	*niku-sashi, hoko*	nee'koo-sah'shee, hoh'-[koh
glass (tumbler)	*koppu*	kohp'poo
kettle	*tetsubin*	teh-tsoo'been
knife	*hōchō, naifu*	h*oh'*ch*oh*, ni'foo
oven	*sutobu*	sootoh'boo

English.	Japanese (romanized).	Pronunciation.
plate	*sara*	sah'rah
saucepan, pot	*nabe*	nah'beh
saucer	*uke-zara*	oo'keh-zah-rah
serviette	*kuchi-fuki*	koo'chee-foo'kee
spoon	*saji*	sah'jee
—, table-	*okii-saji*	oh-k*ee*'-sah'jee
—, tea-	*cha-saji*	chah-sah'jee
table-cloth	*teburu-kake*	teh-boo'roo-kah'keh
tea-pot	*dobin*	dohbeen'
tray	*bon*	bohn
wineglass	*saka-dzuki*	sah'kah-dzoo'kee

15. Dress and Dressing. (*Ifu ku nado.*)

(See also Vocabulary 16, and Shopping, p. 101.)

English.	Japanese (romanized).	Pronunciation.
Bracelet	*udewa*	oodeh'wah
braces	*zubon-dzuri*	dzoo'bohn-dzoo'ree
brooch	*eri-dome*	eh'ree-doh'meh
brush	*burashĭ*	boorah'sh'
button	*botan*	boh'tahn
button-hook	*botan-kake*	boh'tahn-kah'keh
calico	*mempu*	mem'poo
cap	*shappu*	shahp'poo
cloak, cape	*kappa*	kahp'pah [sh'
clothes-brush	*kimono no burashĭ*	keemoh'noh noh boorah'-
coat	*kimono, kotto*	keemoh'noh, koht-toh
comb	*kushi*	koo'shee
cotton	*momen*	moh'men
dress (lady's)	*onna-no-kimono*	ohn'nah-noh-keemoh'noh
dressing-gown	*yukata*	yoo-kah-tah
evening-dress	*reifuku*	ray-foo'koo
flannel	*fūraneru*	f'rah-neh'roo
flannelette	*men-neru*	men-neh'roo
gaiters	*kyahan*	kee-ah'hahn
garters	*tabi-dome*	tah'bee-doh'meh
gloves	*te-bukuro*	teh-bookoo'roh
hair-pin	*kanzashi*	kahn-zah'shee
hat	*bōshi*	bo*h*'shee
jewellery	*kin-gin-zaiku*	keen-ngheen-zi'koo
lace	*reisu*	ray'soo
linen	*rinneru*	reen-neh'roo

English.	Japanese (romanized).	Pronunciation.
muslin	*kanreisha*	kahn-ray'shah
necktie	*erikazari, nekitai*	eh-reekah-zah'ree, neh- [kee-*ti*'
needle	*hari*	hah'ree
overcoat	*gwaito*	g(w)*i*'toh
parasol	*hi-gasa*	hee-ngah'sah
pins	*tome-bari*	toh'meh-bah'ree
pocket	*kakushi*	kah-koo'shee
purse	*kane-ire, saifu*	kah'neh-ee'reh, s*i*'foo
rain-coat; water- [proof	*ama-gappa*	ah'mah-ngahp'pah
razor	*kami-sori*	kah'mee-soh'ree
ring	*yubiwa*	yoobee'wah
scissors	*hasami*	hahsah'mee
silk	*kinu*	kee'noo
skirt	*suso*	soo'soh
soap	*shabon*	shah'bohn
tooth-brush	*haburashi*	hah-boorah'shee
towel	*tenugui*	teh-noo-ngoo'ee
trousers	*zubon*	dzoo'bohn
umbrella	*kōmori-gasa*	k*oh*'mohree-gah'sah
— (Japanese)	*kasa*	kah'sah
watch	*kwai-chiū-dokei*	k(w)*i*-chee*oo*'-doh-kay'
wool	*rasha, ke*	rah'shah, keh

16. Washing List. (*Sentaku Kuchigaki.*)

N.B.—To express "lady's," prefix "*fujin no*" (foo'jeen noh).
" " "children's," " "*kodomo no*" (kohdoh'moh noh).
" " "silk," " "*kinu no*" (kee'noo noh).
" " "woollen," " "*ke no*" (keh noh).
" " "cotton," " "*momen no*" (moh'men noh).

Aprons, pinafores	*mae-kake, hiza-kake*	mah'eh- (*or* hee'zah-) [kah'keh
bath-, dressing- [gowns	*yūkata*	y*oo*'kah-tah
blankets	*furanketto*	foorahnket'toh
bodices	*bojisu*	boh-jee'soo
caps	*shappo*	shahp'poh
chemises	*onna jiban*	ohn'nah jee'bahn
collars, linen	*kara*	kah'rah
—, lace	*kara no reisu*	kah'rah noh ray'soo
coverlets	*nedai kake*	neh-d*i*' kah'keh
cuffs	*kafusu*	kah-foo'soo
drawers	*shita-momohiki*	shee'tah-mohmohhee'kee

English.	Japanese (romanized).	Pronunciation.
dresses, gowns	*onna no kimono*	ohn'nah noh keemoh'noh
flannel waistcoats	*fŭraneru no chokki*	f'rah-neh'roo noh chohk'-
		kee [neh-kee-*ti*
neckties	*eri-kazari, nekitai*	eh'ree-kahzah'ree,
night-dresses	*nemaki*	neh-mah'kee
petticoats	*onna no shita-gi*	ohn'nah noh sheetah'ngee
pillow-cases	*makura-bukuro*	mahkoo'rah bookoo'roh
pocket-handker-	*hanafuki, hankechi*	hahnahfoo'kee, hahnkeh-
serviettes [chiefs	*kuchi-fuki*	koo'chee-foo'kee [chee
sheets	*shiitsŭ*	sh*ee*ts'
shirts [jamas)	*jiban*	jee'bahn
sleeping-suits (py-	*nemaki*	neh-mah'kee
socks (pairs)	*kutsu-shĭta*	koo'tsoo-sh'tah
stockings „	*naga-kutsu-shĭta*	nah'ngah-kootsoo-sh'tah
table-cloths	*teburu-kake*	tehboo'roo-kah'keh
towels	*tenugui*	tehnoo-ngoo'ee
under-vests	*shita-jiban*	sheetah'-jeebahn'

17. House and Furniture. (*Iye to Dōgu.*)

(See also Vocabulary 11, page 25, and Shopping, page 101.)

Arm-chair	*hiji-kake-isu*	hee'jee-kah'keh-ee'soo
basket	*kago*	kah'ngoh
bed	*ne-dai*	neh-*di'*
bedroom	*ne-ma*	neh-mah
bell	*rin*	reen
blind	*mado-kake*	mahdoh-kahkeh
book-case	*honbako*	hohnbah'koh
box	*hako*	hah'koh
broom	*hōki*	h*oh'*kee
candle	*rōsoku*	r*oh'*soh-koo
candlestick	*te-shoku*	teh-shoh'koo
carpet	*jū-tan, mōsen*	j*oo*-tahn, m*oh'*sen
ceiling	*tenjō*	tenj*oh'*
cellar	*ana-gura*	ah'nah-ngoo'rah
chair	*isu*	ee'soo
chest of drawers	*tansu*	tahn'soo
chimney	*kemu-dashi*	keh'moo-dah'shee
clock	*tokei*	toh-kay'
closet (w.c.)	*benjo*	ben'joh
coal	*sekitan*	seh-kee'tahn

English.	Japanese (romanized).	Pronunciation.
counterpane	*ne-dai no uwa-kake*	neh-d*i*' noh oo'wah-kah'keh
cupboard	*to-dana*	toh-dah'nah
curtains	*maku, to bari*	mah'koo, toh bah'ree
cushion	*zabuton*	zahboo'tohn
dining-hall	*shoku-do*	shoh'koo-doh
dining-room	*shokujii no ma*	shoh-kooj*ee*' noh mah
door	*to*	toh
drawing-room	*kyaku no ma*	kee-ah'koo noh mah
electric light	*denki-to*	den'kee-toh
fender	*hiyoke*	hee-yoh'keh
floor	*yuka*	yoo'kah
garden	*niwa*	nee'wah
grate (fire-)	*stobu*	stoh'boo
key	*kagi*	kah'nghee
kitchen	*daidokoro*	d*i*-dohkoh'roh
lamp	*rampu*	rahm'poo
larder	*niku-beya*	nee'koo-beh'yah
library	*shosai*	shoh-s*i*'
light	*akari*	ah-kah'ree
lock	*jōmae*	j*oh*'mah-eh
looking-glass	*kayami*	kah-ngah'mee
matches	*machi*	mah'chee
passage	*rōka*	r*oh*'kah
piano	*piyano*	pee-yah'noh
picture	*gaku*	gah'koo
pillow	*makura*	mahkoo'rah
poker	*hikaki*	heekah'kee
roof	*yane*	yah'neh
room	*heya, zashiki*	heh'yah, zah-shee'kee
seat	*seki, za*	seh'kee, zah
sheets	*uwa-shiki, shiitsŭ*	oo'wah shee'kee, sh*ee*'ts'
shovel	*shabah*	shah'bah
sideboard	*tana*	tah'nah
staircase	*hashigodan*	hah-shee-ngoh'dahn
stairs	*hashigo*	hah-shee'ngoh
table	*teburu*	teh-boo'roo
table-cloth	*teburu kake*	teh-boo'roo kah'keh
tiles	*kawara*	kahwah'rah
tongs	*hi-basami*	hee-bahsah'mee
verandah	*engawa*	en-ngah'wah

English.	Japanese (romanized).	Pronunciation.
wall	*kabe*	kah'beh
wardrobe	*i-fuku todana*	ee-foo'koo tohdah'nah
window	*mado*	mah'doh

18. Religion. (*Shū-kyō.*)

Almighty God	*Zennō no kami*	zenn*oh'* noh kah'mee
altar	*saidan*	s*i'*dahn
angel	*ten-nin*	ten-neen
apostle	*apostoro*	ah-pos-toh'roh
baptise, to	*senrei wo okonau*	sen-ray' woh ohkoh-now'
baptism	*senrei*	sen-ray'
believe, to	*shinkō-suru*	sheenk*oh'*-soo'roo
believer	*shinja*	sheen'jah
bible	*seisho, baiburu*	say'shoh, b*i'*boo-roo
Bible Society	*seisho gwaisha*	say'shoh g(w)*i'*shah
burial	*sō-rei*	s*oh*-ray
cemetery	*haka-sho, bodai-sho*	hah'kah-shoh, boh-d*i'*-[shoh
charity (love)	*ai*	*i*
Christian	*kirisŭto-shinja*	keeree's'toh-sheen'jah
Christianity	*kirisŭto-kyō*	keeree's'toh-kee-*oh*
church (believers)	*kyō-kwai*	kee-*oh'*-k(w)*i*
clergyman	*bōzu, senkyō-shi*	b*oh*-dzoo, sen-k*oh*-shee
Commandments, [the	*jik-kai*	jeek-ki
Communion	*seisan-shĭki*	say-sahn-sh'kee
conscience	*honshin*	hohn-sheen
conversion	*kaishin*	k*i'*sheen
Creator, Maker	*Zō-butsŭ-sha*	dz*oh'*boots'-shah
Cross, the	*jūjika*	j*oo'*jeekah
death	*shi*	shee
devil	*akuma*	ahkoo'mah
divine	*kami no*	kah'mee noh
duty	*gimu*	ghee'moo
epistle	*fumi*	foo'mee
eternal, everlasting	*ei-kyū, no*	ay-kee-*oo*, noh
eternal life	*ei-kyū no inochi*	ay-kee-*oo* noh ee-noh'-[chee
evil (*adj.*)	*warui, ashiki*	wah-roo'ee, ah-shee'kee
evil (*n.*)	*aku*	ah'koo
faith	*shinkō*	sheenk*oh'*
faithful (*adj.*)	*makoto naru, shin-jitsu naru*	mahkoh'toh nah'roo, sheen-jeet'soo nah'roo

English.	Japanese (romanized).	Pronunciation.
forgive, to	*yurusu*	yoo-roo'soo
forgiveness	*yurushi, kamben*	yoo-roo'shee, kahm'ben
glory	*kagayaki*	kah-ngah-yah'kee
God	*Kami, Tenshū*	kah'mee, ten'sh'
goodness	*zen-ji*	zen-jee
gospel	*fuku-in*	foo'koo-een
grace	*megumi*	meh-ngoo'mee
happiness	*kwairaku*	k(w)*i*-rah'koo
heart	*kokoro*	kohkoh'roh
heaven	*ten*	ten
hell (Gehenna)	*jigoku*	jee-ngoh'koo
-- (Hades)	*yomiji*	yoh-mee'jee
holiness	*shinsei*	sheensay'
holy spirit	*seirei*	sayray'
hope	*nozomi*	noh-zoh'mee
humility	*kenson*	ken'sohn
hymn	*sambi-ka*	sahm'bee-kah
hymn-book	*sambi-ka bon*	sahm'bee-kah bohn
immortality	*eisei*	aysay'
infinite	*saigen naki*	s*i*'nghen nah'kee
intercessor	*kwankai*	k(w)ahn-k*i*'
Jesus Christ	*Yaso Kirisūto*	yah'soh keeree's'toh
justice [ven	*seigi*	say'nghee
Kingdom of Hea-	*ten-koku*	ten-koh'koo
Lamb of God	*Kami no ko-hitsuji*	kah'mee noh koh-hee-
life	*inochi*	eenoh'chee [tsoo'jee
Lord	*Shu*	shoo
Lord's Supper	*Shu no ban-san*	shoo noh bahn-sahn
love	*itsukushimi*	eetsookooshee'mee
lust	*niku-yoku*	nee'koo-yoh'koo
mass (Christian)	*dai-hō-e*	d*i*-h*oh*-eh
— (Buddhist)	*tsuizen*	tsoo-ee-zen
mediator	*kwankai*	k(w)ahn-k*i*
meekness	*kenson*	ken-sohn
mercy	*megumi*	meh-ngoo'mee
minister	*kwaishi*	k(w)*i*'shee [nghee
miracle	*shimpen, fushigi*	sheem'pen, foo-shee'-
missionary	*senkyō-shi*	senkee-*oh*'shee
morality	*dōtoku*	d*oh*'tohkoo
mortal	*shinu beki*	shee'noo beh'kee

English.	Japanese (romanized).	Pronunciation.
New Testament	*shin-yaku Zen-sho*	sheen-yah'koo zen-shoh
obedience	*shitagau-koto*	sheetah'ngow-koh'toh
offertory	*kenkin*	ken-keen
Old Testament	*kyūyaku Zen-sho*	kee-*oo*'yahkoo zen-shoh
parable	*tatoe-banashi*	tahtoh'eh-bah-nah'shee
pardon	*yurushi*	yooroo'shee
peace	*anraku*	ahn-rah'koo
pity	*awaremi*	ahwahreh'mee
praise	*homare*	hohmah'reh
prayer	*inori*	ee-noh'ree
priest	*bōzu*	bo*h*'dzoo
Protestant	*shin-kyō-to*	sheen-kee-*oh*-toh
Protestantism	*shin-kyō*	sheen-kee-*oh*'
Providence	*shin-sei*	sheen-say
pulpit	*kōdan*	ko*h*'dahn
purity	*keppaku*	kep-pah'koo
reconciliation	*yawaragi*	yah-wah-rah'nghee
Redeemer	*Kyū-sei-shu*	kee-*oo*'-say-shoo
redemption	*kyū-sei*	kee-*oo*'-say
religion	*shūkyō*	sh*oo*-kee-*oh*
repentance	*kō-kai*	ko*h*-ki
resurrection	*fukkwatsū*	fook-k(w)ah'ts'
righteousness	*gi, sei-gi*	ghee, say'nghee
Roman Catholic	*ten-shu-kyō-to*	ten-shoo-kee*oh*'-toh
Sabbath, the	*ansoku-nichi*	ahnsoh'koo-nee'chee
sacrament	*sakūramento*	sah-k'rahmen'toh
sacred	*sei naru*	say nah'roo
sacrifice	*gi-sei*	ghee-say'
salvation	*sukui, kyū-shō*	sookoo'ee, kee-*oo*-sho*h*
Saviour, the	*Kyū-sei-shu*	kee-*oo*'-say-shoo
Scripture, the	*seisho*	say'shoh
selfishness	*shi-yoku*	shee-yoh'koo
sermon	*sekkyō*	sek-kee-*oh*'
service, divine	*reihai-shiki*	ray-h*i*'-shee'kee
sin	*tsumi*	tsoo'mee
sinner	*tsumi-bito*	tsoo'mee bee'toh
Son of God	*Kami no ko*	kah'mee noh koh
sorrow	*nageki*	nah'ngeh-kee
soul	*tamashii*	tahmahsh*ee*'
Sunday school	*nichiyō-gakko*	neechee-yo*h*'-ngahk'koh

English.	Japanese (romanized).	Pronunciation.
temperance (general)	*tsutsushimi*	tsoo-tsoo-shee'mee
temptation	*yūwaku*	yoo'wahkoo
thankfulness	*kansha*	kahn'shah
tract	*zas-sho*	zahs-shoh
trust	*shinyō*	sheen-y*oh'*
truth	*makoto, shinjitsŭ*	mah-koh'toh, sheenjee'ts'
unbelief	*fu-shin*	foo-sheen
unfaithful	*fu-shinjitsŭ naru*	foo-sheenjee'ts' nah'roo
virtue	*toku*	toh'koo
wicked	*ashiki, aku no*	ah-shee'kee, ah'koo noh
wickedness	*aku*	ah'koo
will	*kokoro, ki-bō*	kohkoh'roh, kee-b*oh*
wisdom	*chi shĭki*	chee sh'kee
Word of God	*kami no kotoba*	kah'mee noh kohtoh'bah
world, the	*sekai, shaba*	seh-k*i'*, shah'bah
worship	*rei-hai*	ray-h*i*
worshipper	*rei-haisha*	rayh*i'*shah

19. Professions, Trades, &c. (*Kagyō, shōbai, nado.*)

(For Shopping see p. 101.)

Actor	*yakusha*	yahkoo-shah
actress	*onna-yakusha*	ohn'nah-yahkoo'shah
architect	*kenchiku-shi*	ken-chee'koo-shee
artist	*ekaki*	eh-kah'kee
baker	*pan-ya*	pahn-yah
banker	*ginkō chō*	gheenk*oh'* ch*oh*
barber	*kami-yui, tokoya*	kah'mee-yoo'ee,toh-koh'-yah
bookseller	*hon-ya*	hohn-yah
butcher	*niku-ya*	nee'koo-yah
carpenter	*daiku*	d*i'*koo
chemist (apothecary)	*kusuri-ya*	koosoo'ree-yah
confectioner	*kwashi-ya*	k(w)ah'shee-yah
cook	*kokku*	kohk'koo
dentist	*ha-isha*	hah-ee'shah
doctor	*isha*	ee'shah
farmer	*hyakŭshō*	hee-ahk'sh*oh'*
fisherman	*ryō-shi*	ree-*oh'*shee
fishmonger	*sakana-ya*	sahkah'nah-yah
florist	*hana-ya*	hah'nah-yah
governess	*jokyō-shi*	joh-kee-*oh'*-shee

English.	Japanese (romanized).	Pronunciation.
greengrocer	*yaoya*	yah-oh'yah
hairdresser (woman's)	*kami-yui*	kah'mee-yoo'ee
hatter	*bōshi-ya*	b*oh*'shee-yah
jeweller	*kazariya*	kahzahree'yah
lawyer	*daigen-nin*	d*i*'ghen-neen
maid-servant	*gejo* (more polite, *jochū*)	gheh'joh (joh-ch*oo*)
messenger	*tsŭkai no mono*	ts(oo)k*i*' noh moh'noh
money-changer	*ryō-gae-ya*	r(ee)y*oh*'-ngah'eh-yah
nurse (female)	*kangojo*	kahngoh'joh
optician	*megane-shi*	meh-ngah'neh-shee
photographer	*sha-shin-ya*	shah-sheen-yah
physician	*isha*	ee'shah
policeman	*junsa*	joon'sah
porter (light)	*karuko*	kahroo'koh
printer	*insatsu-shi*	een-sah'tsoo shee
servant	*hōkōnin*, *meshi-tsukai*	h*oh*k*oh*neen, meh'shee-tsook*i*'
shoemaker	*kutsu-ya*	koo'tsoo-yah
shopkeeper	*akindo*	ahkeen'doh
singer	*utai-ko*	oot*i*'-koh
student	*shosei*	shoh-say'
surgeon	*gekwa-isha*	geh'k(w)ah-ee'shah
surveyor	*kensa-kan*	ken'sah-kahn
tailor	*shĭtate-ya*	sh'tah'teh-yah
teacher	*kyōshi*, *sensei*, *shishō*	kee-*oh*'shee, sen-say', shee-sh*oh*'
tradesman	*akindo*	ahkeen'doh
watchmaker	*tokeiya*	toh-kay'yah

20. Countries and Nations. (*Sho-koku.*)

(See Travelling, pages 81—87.

Africa	*Afurika (-shū)*	ahfooree'kah (-sh*oo*)
America	*Amerika*	ahmehree'kah
American, an	*Amerika-jin*	ahmehree'kah-jeen
Asia	*Ajia (-shū)*	ah'jeeah (-sh*oo*)
China	*Shina*, *Kara*	shee'nah, kah'rah
Chinaman, a	*Shina-jin*	shee'nah-jeen
England	*Igirisu*, *Eikoku*	ee-ngheeree'soo, aykoh'koo
English (language)	*Igirisu kotoba*, *Eigo*	ee-ngheeree'soo kohtoh'bah, ay'ngoh
Englishman	*Igirisu-jin*, *Eikoku-jin*	ee-ngheeree'soo-jeen, ay-koh'koo-jeen

English.	Japanese (romanised).	Pronunciation.
Europe	*Yōroppa, Seiyō*	yo*h*'rohp-pah, say-yo*h*'
France	*Furansu*	foorahn'soo
Frenchman	*Furansu-jin*	foorahn'soo-jeen
Germany	*Doitsu no hĭto*	doy'tsoo noh sh'toh
German, a	*Doitsu-jin*	doy'tsoo-jeen
Great Britain	*Dai-Buritan*	d*i*-booreetahn'
India	*Indo, Tenjiku*	een'doh, tenjee'koo
Japan	*Nippon, Nihon*	neep'pohn, nee'hohn[jeen
Japanese, a	*Nihon-jin, Nippon-*	neehohn'-jee*n*,neeppohn'-
Russia	*Ro-koku, Rōsha* [*jin*	roh-koh'koo, r*oh*-shah
Russian, a	*Ro-koku-jin*	roh-koh'koo-jeen
Scotland	*Sukottorando*	soo-koht-tohrahn'doh

21. Travelling. (*Ryo-kō.*)

(For Conversations see pages 81—90.)

Arrival	*tō-chaku*	t*oh*-chah'koo
bag	*fukuro*	fookoo'roh
— (hand-)	*kaban*	kah'bahn
berth (on ship)	*ne-doko*	neh-doh'koh
bill (account)	*kanjō*	kahn-j*oh*
boarding-house	*geshuku-ya*	gheh-shoo'koo-yah
boat	*fune, kobune*	foo'neh, kohboo'neh
booking-office	*shussatsŭjo*	shoos-sahts'joh
box	*hako*	hah'koh
carriage, coach	*basha*	bah'shah
change (money)	*tsuri*	tsoo'ree
charge (price)	*ne, nedan*	neh, neh'dahn
class, first	*jōtō*	j*oh*t*oh*
—, second	*chūtō*	choot*oh*
—, third	*katō*	kaht*oh*'
coachman	*gyosha*	ghee-oh'shah
companion	*tābi-zure, michi-zure*	t*ah*bee-dzooreh, meechee-
consul	*ryōji*	ree-oh'jee [dzooreh
cushion	*zabuton*	zahboo'tohn
custom-house [cer	*zeikwan*	zay'k(w)ahn
custom-house offi-	*zei-kwan kwanri*	zay'k(w)ahn k(w)ahn'ree
departure (by land)	*shuttatsu*	shoot-tah'tsoo
— (by water)	*shuppan*	shoop'pahn
distance	*michi-nori, risū*	mee'chee-noh'ree, rees*oo*'
drive, a	*basha-nori*	bah'shah-noh'ree

English.	Japanese (romanized).	Pronunciation.
driver	*gyosha*	ghee-oh'shah
dust (raised by wind)	*hokori*	hohkoh'ree
duty	*zei*	zay
duty-free	*muzei*	moo-zay'
engine	*kikwan-sha*	kee'k(w)ahn-shah
— -driver	*kikwan-shi*	kee'k(w)ahn-shee
expenses (trav.)	*ryokō-hi*	ree-ohk*oh'*-hee
express (train)	*kyūkō ressha*	kee-*oo'*k*oh* res'shah
fare (charge)	*chinsen*	cheen'sen
good-bye	*sayōnara*	sah-y*oh'*nahrah
guard (railway)	*sha-chō*	shah-ch*oh*
guidance	*annai*	ahn-n*i'*
guide, a	*annaisha*	ahn-n*i'*shah
guide-book	*annai-sho*	ahn-n*i'*-shoh
hotel, inn	*yadoya, hoteru*	yahdoh'yah, hoh-teh-roo
inspector	*kensa-nin*	ken'sah-neen
interpreter	*tsūben, tsūji*	ts*oo'*ben, ts*oo'*jee
journey	*tabi, ryokō*	tah'bee, ree-ohk*oh'*
junction (railway)	*tetsudō no kōsaten*	teh-tsood*oh'* noh k*oh*-sah-ten
key	*kagi*	kah'nghee
label (tag)	*fuda*	foo'dah
landlady	*okami-san*	ohkah'mee-sahn
landlord (hotel)	*teishiū*	tay-shee'(oo)
lavatory	*chōzu-ba, benjo*	ch*oh*-dzoo-bah, ben'joh
luggage, baggage	*nimotsu*	neemoh'tsoo
— -van (rail.)	*kisha no ni-guruma*	kee'shah noh nee-gooroo'-mah
match (for light)	*machi, haya-tsūkegi*	mah'chee, hah'yah-ts(oo)-keh'nghee
money-changer	*ryō-gae-ya*	ree-*oh'*-ngah'eh-yah
money, ready-	*genkin*	ghen'keen
newspaper	*shimbunshi*	sheemboon'shee
office	*jimusho, yakŭsho*	jeemoo'shoh, yah'k'shoh
official	*shĭkwan, yakunin*	sh'k(w)ahn', yahkoo'neen
omnibus	*nori-ai basha*	noh'ree-*i* bah'shah
package	*tsutsumi*	tsoo-tsoo'mee
party (pleasure-)	*yu san*	yoo sahn
passenger	*nori-kyaku*	nohree-kee-ah'koo
passport	(*ryokō-*) *menjō*	[ree-ohk*oh'*-] menj*oh'*
payment	*harai*	hahr*i'*
pier	*hatoba*	hah-toh'bah

English.	Japanese (romanised).	Pronunciation.
pipe (tobacco-)	*kiseru*	keeseh'roo
policeman	*junsa*	joon'sah
porter (rail.)	*eki-fu*	eh'kee-foo
— (light)	*karuko*	kahroo'koh
portmanteau	*kaban*	kah'bahn
price (cost)	*nedan, atai, ne*	neh'dahn, ah*ti'*, neh
purse	*kane-ire, kinchaku*	kah'neh-ee'reh, keen- [chah'koo
railway	*tetsūdō*	teh-ts(oo)d*oh'*
— -carriage	*tetsūdō kyakusha*	teh-ts(oo)d*oh'* kee-ah-koo'shah
receipt	*uke-tori*	oo'keh-toh'ree
restaurant	*ryōri-ya*	ree-*oh'*ree-yah
road, way	*michi*	mee'chee
rug	*ketto*	ket'toh
saddle	*kura*	koo'rah
ship	*fune*	foo'neh
station	*sūteshon, teisha-ba*	s'teh'shohn, tay'shah- [bah
station-master	*eki-chō*	eh'kee-ch*oh*
steamer	*jōkisen*	j*oh'*keesen
stirrup	*abumi*	ahboo'mee
telescope	*tō-megane, bōenkyō*	t*oh*-meh-ngah'neh, b*oh*- [en-kee-*oh*
ticket	*kippu*	keep'poo
—, return	*ōfuku-gippu*	*oh*fookoo-ngheep'poo
time-table	*jikan hyō*	jee'kahn hee-*oh*
tip (gratuity)	*sakate*	sahkah'teh
train (rail.)	*kisha, ressha*	kee'shah, res'shah
tram	*tetsūdō-basha*	teh-ts(oo)d*oh'*-bah'shah
traveller	*ryo-jin, tabi-bito*	ree-oh-jeen, tah'bee- [bee'toh
trunk	*kaban*	kahbahn'
tunnel	*tonneru*	tohn-neh'roo
waiter	*bōi, kyūji*	b*oh'*ee, kee-*oo'*jee
waiting-room	*machi-ai-ba*	mah'chee-*i*-bah
saloon	*chabuya* (vulg.)	chahboo'yah
voyage	*kōkai*	k*oh'*ki

22. Ships and Shipping. (*Fune Nado.*)

(For Conversations, see page 85.)

Anchor	*ikari*	eekah'ree
berth	*ne-doko*	neh-doh'koh
boat (ship)	*fune*	foo'neh
bow	*he-saki*	heh-sah'kee

English.	Japanese (romanized).	Pronunciation.
cabin	*kyaku-shitsŭ, funa-*	kee-ah'koo-shee'ts', foo'
captain	*senchō* [*beya*	sen-choh [nah-beh'yah
compass	*jishaku*	jee-shah'koo
crew	*nori-kumi*	noh'ree-koo'mee
deck	*kampan*	kahm'pahn
flag	*hata*	hah'tah
helm (rudder)	*kaji*	kah'jee
landing-stage	*hatoba*	hah-toh'bah
life-buoy	*uki*	oo'kee
light-house	*tō-myō-dai*	to*h*-m'yo*h*-d*i*
mast	*ho-bashira*	hoh-bahshee'rah
oar	*ro ; kai* (scull)	roh, k*i* [shah
pilot	*midzu saki annai-*	mee'dzoo sah'kee ahnn*i*'-
port (harbour)	*minato* [*sha*	meenah'toh
porthole	*mado*	mah'doh
— (for gun)	*hō-mon*	ho*h*'mohn
rope	*nawa*	nah'wah
sail	*ho*	hoh
seaman (sailor)	*suifu, funa-ko*	soo'eefoo, foo'nah-koh
sea-sickness	*funa-yoi*	foo'nah-yoy
ship	*fune*	foo'neh
steamboat	*jōki-sen*	jo*h*'kee-sen
steersman	*kaji-tori*	kah'jee-toh'ree
stern	*tomo, sem-bi*	toh'moh, sem-bee
steward	*makanai-kata*	mahkahn*i*'-kah'tah

23. Trade and Commerce. (*Shō-gyo.*)

(For Conversations see pages 103—106.)

English.	Japanese (romanized).	Pronunciation.
Accept, to (bill)	*hiki-ukeru*	hee'kee-ookeh'roo
acceptor	*hike-uke-nin*	hee'kee-oo'keh-neen
account	*kanjō*	kahnjo*h*' [roo
—, to close	*kanjō wo shimeru*	kahnjo*h*' woh sheemeh'-
—, to settle an	*kes-san-suru*	kes-sahn-soo'roo
—, current	*kōgyo keisan*	ko*h*'ngoh kay'sahn
—, on joint	*nori-ai-de*	noh'ree-*i*-deh
accountant	*kanjō-kata*	kahn-jo*h*'-kah'tah
address	*shuku-sho*	shoo'koo-shoh
advance (money)	*mae-gashi*	mah'eh-ngah'shee
advice, letter of	*annai-jō*	ahn-n*i*'-jo*h*
affidavit	*sei-gen, sen-sei*	say-nghen, sen-say'

English.	Japanese (romanized).	Pronunciation.
after date	*hidzuke-go*	hee-dzoo'keh-ngoh
— sight	*ichi-ran-go*	ee'chee-rahn-ngoh
agent	*dai-ri-nin*	d*i*-ree-neen
agreement	*keiyaku*	kay-yah'koo
arrears	*todo-kōri-kin*	toh'doh-k*oh*'ree-keen
assets [tee)	*zaisan*	z*i*'sahn
assurance (guaran-	*hoshō*	hoh-sh*oh*'
attorney (lawyer)	*daigen-nin*	d*i*-ghen-neen
auditor	*kwaikei-kensa-nin*	k(w)*i*-kay'-kensah-neen
balance	*zankin*	zahn-keen
— -sheet	*kei-san-hyō*	kay-sahn-hee-*oh*
bank	*ginkō*	gheenk*oh*'
banking	*ginkō-ei-gyō*	gheenk*oh*'-ay-nghee-*oh*
bank-note	*ginkō-shihei*	gheenk*oh*'-shee-hay'
bankrupt	*hasan-nin*	hah'sahn-neen
bankruptcy	*hasan*	hah'sahn
bearer [tion)	*jisan-nin*	jee'sahn-neen
bill (accommoda-	*yūdzū-tegata*	yoodz*oo*-teh-ngah'tah
bill of exchange	*kawase-tegata*	kahwah'seh-teh-ngah'tah
— of lading	*funadzumi-shōsho*	foonah-dzoo'mee-sh*oh*'-shoh
bond (security)	*shaku-yō-shōsho*	shah'koo-y*oh*-sh*oh*'shoh
book-keeper	*boki-kata*	boh'kee-kah' tah
brokerage	*kōsen*	k*oh*'sen
business	*akinai, shōbai*	ah-kee-n*i*', sh*oh*'b*i*
buyer (customer)	*kai-te*	k*i*-teh
cable address	*denshin-na-ate*	den'sheen-nah-ah'teh
— -gram	*dempō*	demp*oh*'
—, to	*denshin wo utsu*	den'sheen woh oo'tsoo
capital	*shihon*	shee'hohn
cargo	*tsumi-ni*	tsoo'mee-nee
carriage (cost of)	*un-chin*	oon-cheen [bahr*i*'
carriage forward	*unsō-chin saki-barai*	oon-s*oh*'-cheen sah'kee-
carriage-(post-)paid	*unsō-chin zumi*	oon-s*oh*'-cheen dzoo'mee
cash sale	*gen-kin-uri*	ghen-keen-oo'ree
catalogue	*mokuroku*	mohkooroh'koo [joh
chamber of com-	*shō-gyō-kaigi-jo*	sh*oh*-nghee-*oh*-k*i*'nghee-
cheque, a [merce	*ko-gitte*	koh-ngheet'teh
cheque, crossed	*ōsen-ko-gitte*	*oh*'sen-koh-ngheet'teh
clearing-house (cus- [toms)	*kō-kanjo*	k*oh*-kahn'joh

English.	Japanese (romanized).	Pronunciation.
clerk	*ban-to*	bahn-toh
commerce	*bōeki*	boh'eh-kee
company, a joint-stock	*gō-mei kwaisha*	goh-may k(w)i'shah
—, a limited	*yūgen-sekinin-kwai-sha*	yoo'nghen-sehkee'neen-k(w)i'shah
consign, to	*okuru*	ohkoo'roo
consignee	*ni-uke-nin*	nee-oo'keh-neen
consignment	*...-okuri-ni*	...-ohkoo'ree-nee
consignor	*...-okuri-nin*	...-ohkoo'ree-neen
contra account	*hantai kanjō*	hahnti' kahnjoh'
contract, a	*yakujo*	yahkoo'joh
cost	*ne dan*	nehdahn
cost, insurance and freight (c.i.f.)	*tōchaku daika*	toh'chahkoo di'kah
cost price	*genka*	ghen-kah
credit balance	*zan-kin*	zahn-keen
creditor	*sai-shu*	si-shoo
customs' duties	*kwan-zei*	k(w)ahn-zay
damages, compensation	*songai-baishō*	sohn-nghi'-bi-shoh'
date, at three months'	*san-ga-getsu nichigen de*	sahn-ngah-nget'soo nee'chee-ngen deh
debt	*kari, shakkin*	kah'ree, shahk'keen
debtor	*kari-te*	kah'ree-teh
deliver, to	*sashi-watasu*	sah'shee-wah-tah'soo
demurrage	*taisen-hi-yō*	ti'-sen-hee-yoh
directors	*tori-shimari*	toh'ree-sheemah'ree
discount	*wari-biki*	wah'ree-bee'kee
—, to	*wari-biki suru*	wah'ree-bee'kee soo'roo
dividend	*haitō-kin*	hitoh'-keen
dock	*senkyō-jo, dokku*	sen-keeoh'-joh, dohk'koo
dock and harbour dues	*dokku nyū-kō-zei*	dohk'koo n'yoo-koh-zay
double entry	*fuku-shiki-boki-hō*	foo'koo-shee'kee-boh'kee-hoh
draw, to (bill)	*kawase wo torikumu*	kahwah'seh woh tohree-koo'moo
drawee	*shiharai-nin*	shee-hah-ri'-neen
drawer (of bill)	*furi dashi nin*	foo'ree dah'shee neen
duty	*kwan-zei*	kwahn-zay'
—, export	*yushutsū-zei*	yooshoo'ts'-zay
— -free	*mu-zei*	moo-zay'

English.	Japanese (romanized).	Pronunciation.
duty, import	*yu-nyū-zei*	yoo-nee-*oo'*-zay
—, liable to	*ni kakawaru*	nee kah-kah-wah'roo [ree
estimate, an	*yo-san, mitsumori*	yoh'sahn, meetsoomoh-'
exchange (monetary)	*ryōgae*	ree-*oh'*ngah-eh
export (-ation)	*yushutsŭ*	yooshoo'ts'
export, to	*yushutsŭ suru*	yooshoo'ts' soo'roo
exchange (mart)	*torihiki-jo*	tohreehee'kee-joh
firm, a	*shōsha, shōten*	sh*oh'*shah, sh*oh'*ten
free on board (f.o.b.)	*funa-zumi-daika*	foo'nah-dzoo'mee-d*i*'kah
freight (charge)	*unsō-chin*	oons*oh'*-cheen
— -ship	*funa-chin*	foo'nah-cheen
goods	*nimotsŭ*	neemoh'ts'
gross weight	*fūtai*	*foo-ti*
guarantee	*hoshō*	hoh-sh*oh'* [neen
guarantor	*hoshō-nin, uke-nin*	hoh-sh*oh*-neen, oo'keh-
holder (of bill)	*shoji-nin*	shoh'jee-neen
import	*yu-nyū*	yoo-nee-*oo'*
import, to	*yu-nyū suru*	yoo-nee-*oo'* soo'roo
import trade	*yu-nyū-shō-gyō*	yoo-nee-*oo'*-sh*oh*-ng'y*oh*
importer	*yu-nyū-nin*	yoo-nee-oo'-neen
indemnity	*shōkin*	sh*oh'*keen [roo
indorse, to	*uragaki wo suru*	oorah-ngah'kee woh soo'-
indorsement	*uragaki*	oorah-ngah'kee
indorsee	*hi-uragaki-nin*	hee-oorah-ngah'kee-neen
indorser [ment)	*uragaki-nin*	oorah-ngah'kee-neen
instalment (of pay-	*nashi kuzushi*	nah'shee koodzoo'shee
insurance company	*hoken-gwaisha*	hoh'ken-ng(w)*i*'shah
—, fire	*kwasai-hoken*	kwahs*i*'-hoh'ken
—, marine	*kaijō-hoken*	k*i*-j*oh'*-hoh'ken
— policy	*hoken-shōsho*	hoh'ken-sh*oh'*shoh
— premium	*hoken-ryō*	hoh'ken-ree-*oh'*
insure, to	*hoken suru*	hoh'ken soo'roo
interest (rate of)	*rishi, risoku*	ree'shee, ree-soh'koo
invoice	*okurijō*	ohkooreej*oh'*
I.O.U.	*shakuyō-shōsho*	shahkoo-y*oh'*-sh*oh'* shoh
landing charges	*riku-age-chin*	ree'koo-ah'ngeh-cheen
liabilities	*fusai*	foos*i'*
lighterage	*ni-bune-chin*	nee-boo'neh-cheen
liquidation (wind-	*seisan*	say'sahn
load, to [up)	*tsumi-ni wo suru*	tsoo'mee-nee woh soo'roo

English.	Japanese (romanized).	Pronunciation.
loss	*sonshitsŭ*	sohnshee'ts'
mail-day	*yūbin-sen shime-kiri no hi*	yoo'been-sen shee'meh-kee'ree noh hee
manufacture, to	*seizō-suru*	say-z*oh*'-soo'roo
manufactured goods	*sei-hin*	say-heen
manufacturer	*seizō-sha*	say-z*oh*'-shah
market (for goods)	*muki*	moo'kee
— -price	*sōba*	s*oh*'bah
— -place	*ichi-ba*	ee'chee-bah
merchandise	*shō-hin*	sh*oh*'-heen
merchant	*shōnin, akindo*	sh*oh*'neen, ah-keen'doh
merchant ship	*shōsen*	sh*oh*'sen
money	*kinsen*	keen'sen
money-market	*kinyu shijō*	keen'yoo shee-j*oh*'
negotiable	*yuzuri-watashi no dekiru*	yoo-dzoo'ree-wah-tah'-shee noh deh-kee'roo
negotiate, to (business)	*kake-au*	kah'keh-ow
net cost	*gen-ka*	ghen-kah
— profit	*rieki, mōke*	ree-eh'kee, m*oh*'keh
— weight	*shōmi*	sh*oh*'mee
obligation (debt)	*fusai*	foos*i*'
order, an	*chūmon*	ch*oo*'mohn
—, to	*chūmon wo suru*	ch*oo*'mohn woh soo'roo
package (case)	*hako*	hah'koh
packing	*nidzukuri*	needzookoo'ree
paid	*harai-zumi*	hah-r*i*'-dzoo'mee
par	*dōka*	d*oh*'kah
— of exchange	*kawase no dōka*	kahwah'seh noh d*oh*'kah
partner	*sha-in*	shah-een
partnership	*kumi-ai*	koo'mee-*i*
payable	*harai-watasu-beki*	hahr*i*'-wahtah'soo-beh'-kee
payee	*uketori-nin*	ookehtoh'ree-neen
payment	*shi-harai*	shee-hahr*i*'
per annum	*mai-nen, nen ni*	m*i*-nen, nen nee
per cent., 2½	*ni bu go rin*	nee boo goh reen
— —, 3	*sam bu*	sahm boo
port of delivery	*moku-teki-kō*	moh'koo-teh'kee-k*oh*
port dues	*minato zei*	meenah'toh zay
price, cost-	*shi-ire, moto-ne*	shee-ee'reh, moh'toh-neh
— -list	*daika-hyō*	d*i*'kah-hee-*oh*

English.	Japanese (romanized).	Pronunciation.
price, selling	*uri-ne*	oo'ree-neh
—, trade	*dōgyō-nin dōshi no nedan*	d*oh*-ngeeo*h*'-neen d*oh*'shee noh neh'dahn
—, wholesale	*oroshi uri no nedan*	ohroh'shee oo'ree noh neh'dahn
proceeds	*uri-age daka*	oo'ree-ah'ngheh-dah'kah
profit	*toku, rieki*	toh'koo, ree-eh'kee
— and loss account	*son toku kanjō*	sohn toh'koo kahnj*oh'*
promissory note	*yakusoku tegata*	yahkoosoh'koo teh-ngah'-tah
prospectus	*shui-sho*	shoo'ee-shoh
punctual	*kichōmen na*	keech*oh*'men nah
purchase, to	*kau*	kow
quality (of goods)	*hin shitsŭ*	heen shee'ts'
quantity	*taka*	tah'kah
quarter (3 months)	*san-ga-getsŭ*	sahn-ngah-geh'ts'
quotation (of price)	*ii-ne*	*ee*-neh
quote, to	*ne wo tsukeru*	neh woh tsookeh'roo
rate of exchange	*kawase*	kahwah'seh
receipt	*uketori-shō*	ookehtoh'ree-sh*oh*
reduction	*ne-biki*	neh-bee'kee
re-export	*sai-yushutsŭ*	s*i*-yooshoo'ts'
references	*shinyō shōkai-nin*	sheen-y*oh'* sh*oh*'k*i*-neen
register, to (letter)	*kakitome ni suru*	kahkeetoh'meh nee soo'-roo
registered letter	*kakitome no tegami*	kahkeetoh'meh noh teh-ngah'mee
registration	*kakitome*	kahkeetoh'meh
— fee	*kakitome ryō*	kahkeetoh'meh ree-*oh*
remittance	*sōkin*	s*oh*'keen
rent	*ya-chin*	yah-cheen
reply	*henji, hentō*	hen'jee, hen-t*oh'*
—, to	*henji suru*	hen'jee soo'roo
representative	*dairi-nin*	d*i*'ree-neen
retail	*ko-uri no*	koh-oo'ree noh
—, to	*ko-uri wo suru*	koh-oo'ree woh soo'roo
salary	*gekkyū*	ghek-kee-*oo'*
sale	*uru koto*	oo'roo koh'toh
salesman (seller)	*uri-te, uri-kata*	oo'ree-teh, oo'ree-kah'tah
sample	*mihon*	mee'hohn
security (guarantee)	*hoshō*	hoh-sh*oh'*
sell, to	*uru*	oo'roo
settling days	*uke-watashi no hi*	oo'keh-wahtah'shee noh hee

English.	Japanese (romanized).	Pronunciation
shareholder	*kabu-nushi*	kah'boo-noo'shee
shares	*kabushiki*	kahbooshee'kee
—, preference	*yū sen kabu*	yoo sen kah'boo
—, railway	*tetsudō-kabu*	teh-tsoodoh'-kah'boo
shipping charges	*funadzumi nyū hi* [*ya*	foonahdzoo'mee nee-oo' hee [sen-yah
shipping house	*funa-zumi shūsen-*	foo'nah-dzoo'mee shoo'-
shipping trade	*kai-un-gyō*	ki-oon-nghee-oh'
solvent	*shiryoku no aru*	shee-ree-oh'koo noh [ah'roo
stock (goods)	*ari ni*	ah'ree nee
stock (shares, etc.)	*kabushiki*	kahbooshee'kee
stock-broker	*kabushiki-nakagai-nin* [*jo*	kahbooshee'kee-nahkah-nghi'-neen [hee'kee-joh
stock exchange	*kabushiki-tori-hiki-*	kahbooshee'kee-toh'ree-
stock-taking	*tana-oroshi*	tah'nah-ohroh'shee
stowage	*tsumi-oki*	tsoo'mee-oh'kee
tare	*fūtai*	foo'ti
tariff (duties)	*zeisoku*	zaysoh'koo
telegraphic address	*denshin-na-ate*	den'sheen-nah-ah'teh
— code	*dempō no angō*	dem-poh' noh ahn-ngoh'
— remittance	*denshin kawase*	den'sheen kahwah'seh
telephone	*denwa ki*	den'wah kee
— exchange	*denwa kō-kwan-jo*	den'wah koh-k(w)ahn-joh
— number	*denwa no bango*	den'wah noh bahn'ngoh
tender, to	*nyu-satsu suru*	nee'oo-sah'tsoo soo'roo
terms (conditions)	*keiyaku no jōken*	kay-yah'koo noh joh'ken
tonnage	*tonsū*	tohnsoo'
— (dues)	*tonzei*	tohn-zay'
towing charges	*hiki-bune-ryō*	hee'kee-boo'neh-ree-oh'
trade	*shōgyō*	shoh-nghee-oh
trade-mark	*shōhyō*	shoh'hee-oh
transaction	*tori-hiki*	toh'ree-hee'kee
transfer	*yudzuri-watashi*	yoodzoo'ree-wahtah'shee
—, to	*yudzuri-watasu*	yoodzoo'ree-wahtah'soo
traveller (commercial)	*chūmon-tori, tabi-akindo*	choo'mohn-toh'ree, tah'-bee-ah-keen'doh
underwriter	*hoken-sha*	hoh'ken-shah
unloading	*ni-oroshi*	nee-ohroh'shee
value	*atai, ne-uchi*	ah-ti', neh-oo'chee
vessel (ship)	*fune*	foo'neh

English.	Japanese (romanized).	Pronunciation.
voucher	*uke-tori-shō*	oo'keh-toh'ree-sho*h*
warehouse	*kura, dozō*	koo'rah, doh-zo*h'*
warranty	*hoshō*	hohsh*oh'*
weight	*mekata*	mehkah'tah
wharf	*hatoba*	hahtoh'bah
wharfage	*hatoba-zei*	hahtoh'bah-zay
wholesale	*ōuri*	*oh*-oo-ree
— merchant	*oroshi-uri*	ohroh'shee-oo'ree
winding-up	*kwaisha no kaisan*	kw*i*'shah noh k*i*'sahn

24. Correspondence. (*Sho-kan.*)

(For Conversations see page 95.)

Address	*shuku-sho, na-ate*	shoo'koo-shoh,nah-ah'teh
address, to	*ateru*	ah-teh'roo
blotting-paper	*sumi-tori-gami*	soo'mee-toh'ree-ngah'-mee
date	*gappi, hidzuke*	gahp'pee, heedzoo'keh
envelope	*jōbukuro*	j*oh*'bookooroh
ink	*inki, sumi*	een'kee, soo'mee
inkstand	*inki-tsubo*	een'kee-tsoo'boh
letter, note	*sho-jō, tegami*	shoh-j*oh*, teh-ngah'mee
— -box	*yūbin-bako*	y*oo'*been-bah'koh
note-paper	*shokan-shi*	shoh'kahn-shee
pen, steel (nib)	*pen*	pen
—, fountain	*mannen-fude*	man'nen-foo'deh
— -holder	*pen-jiku*	pen-jee'koo
pencil	*empitsū*	em-pee'ts'
penknife	*kaichū-gatana*	k*i*-ch*oo'*-ngah-tah'nah
seal	*in, impan*	een, eempahn'
sealing wax	*fū-rō*	f*oo*-r*oh*
sheet of paper, a	*kami ichi mai*	kah'mee ee'chee m*i*
signature	*kimei*	keemay'
write, to	*kaku*	kah'koo
writing	*kakimono*	kahkeemoh'noh
— -desk	*tsukuye*	tsoo-koo'yeh

25. Post-office, Telegraph and Telephone.

(*Yūbin ; denshin ; denwa.*)

(For Conversations see page 95, and for Postal Rates see page 108.)

Book post	*shomotsu-yūbin*	shoh-moh'ts'-*yoo'*been
destination	*yuku-saki, sempō*	yookoo-sah'kee, semp*oh'*
excess (postage)	*fusokuzei*	foo-soh-koo-zay'

English.	Japanese (romanized).	Pronunciation.
letter post	*sho-kwan-yūbin*	shoh-k(w)ahn-yoo'been
money order	*yūbin-kawase*	yoo'been-kah-wah'seh
newspaper wrapper	*obi-fū*	oh'bee-foo
number (of order)	*bangō*	bahn-ngoh' [been
parcel post	*kodzutsu-mi yūbin*	kohdzoo'tsoo - mee yoo'-
postage stamp	*yūbin-gitte*	yoo'been-ngheet'teh
post-card	*yūbin-hagaki*	yoo'been-hah-ngah'kee
poste-restante	*yūbin-kyoku-azukari*	yoo'been-kee-oh'koo-ah-dzoo-kah'ree
postman	*yūbin-haitatsū-nin*	yoo'been-hi-tah'ts'-neen
postmaster	*yūbin-kyoku-chō*	yoo'been-kee-oh'koo-choh
post-office	*yūbin-kyoku*	yoo'been-kee-oh'koo
post-paid	*yūbin ryō harai-zumi no*	yoo'been ree-oh' hahri'-dzoo'mee noh [roo
prepay, to	*mae barai wo suru*	mah'eh bahri' woh soo'-
register, to (a letter)	*kakitome ni suru*	kahkeetoh'meh nee soo'-roo [teh-ngah'mee
registered letter	*kakitome no tegami*	kahkeetoh'meh noh
reply paid	*hempō-harai-zumi*	hempoh'-hahri'-dzoo'mee
ring up, to	*yobi-dasu*	yoh'bee-dah'soo
telegram	*dempō*	dempoh'
—, cost of	*denshin-ryō*	den'sheen-ree-oh'
telegraph form	*dempō-haku-shi*	dempoh'-hah'koo-shee
— messenger	*dempō-zukai*	dempoh'-dzooki'
— office	*denshin-kyoku*	den'sheen-kee-oh'koo
telegraph, to	*denshin wo kakeru*	den'sheen woh kahkeh'roo
telephone	*denwa*	den'wah
—, to	*denwa wo kakeru*	den'wah woh kahkeh'roo
— call office	*denwa kō-kwan-jo*	den'wah koh-kwahn-joh
— number	*denwa bango*	den'wah bahn'ngoh
weight	*mekata*	mehkah'tah
—, over	*yobun-mekata*	yohboon-mehkah'tah

26. Army and Navy. (*Riku-gun; kai-gun.*)

English.	Japanese (romanized).	Pronunciation.
Adjutant	*fukukwan*	fookoo'k(w)ahn
— -general	*sambō-sō-kwan*	sam-boh-soh-k(w)ahn
admiral	*kaigun-taishō*	ki'ngoon-ti-shoh'
advance, to	*susumu*	soo-soo'moo
aide-de-camp	*denrei-shi*	denray'-shee
alarm, an	*keihō*	kayhoh'

English.	Japanese (romanized).	Pronunciation.
ammunition	*dan-yaku*	dahn-yah'koo
— (small arms)	*shōjū danyaku*	sh*oh*-*joo* dahn-yah'koo
ammunition wagon	*danyaku sha*	dahn-yah'koo shah
anchor	*ikari*	eekah'ree
anchorage	*teihaku-jo*	tayhah'koo-joh
armistice	*kyū-sen*	kee-*oo'*-sen
armour	*yoroi*	yoh-roy'
arms	*bu-ki*	boo-kee
arms, small	*shōjū*	sh*oh'joo*
army	*gunzei*	goon-zay
army-corps	*gundan*	goon'dahn
Army list	*riku-gun meibo*	ree'koo-ngoon may'boh
— Medical Corps	*gunibu*	goonee'boo
army orders	*fukueki shōtei*	fookooeh'kee sh*oh'*tay
artillery (guns)	*tai-hō*	*ti*-h*oh*
artillerymen	*hō-hei*	h*oh'*-hay
attack, an	*kōgeki*	k*oh'*ngeh-kee
—, frontal	*shōmen kōgeki*	sh*oh'*men k*oh'*ngeh-kee
attack, to	*kōgeki suru*	k*oh'*ngeh-kee soo'roo
attention !	*ki wo tsuke !*	kee woh tsoo-keh !
axe	*ono*	oh'noh
band	*gaku-tai*	gah'koo-*ti*
band-master	*gaku-tai-chō*	gah'koo-*ti*-ch*oh*
bandsman	*gaku-shu*	gah'koo-shoo
barracks	*heiei*	hay-ay
barrel (rifle)	*tsu-tsu*	tsoo-tsoo
battalion	*daitai*	d*i*-*ti*
battery	*hō-hei-chū-tai*	h*oh*-hay-ch*oo*-*ti*
battle	*kassen*	kahs-sen
battle-ship	*sentō-kan*	sent*oh'*-kahn
bayonet	*jū-ken*	j*oo*-ken
bayonets ! fix-	*tsuke ken !*	tsoo'keh ken !
bearer company	*eiseitai*	ay-say-*ti'*
bivouac, to	*roei suru*	roh-ay' soo'roo
block (ship's)	*semi*	seh'mee
blockade	*hō-sa*	h*oh*-sah
bomb, -shell	*haretsū-dama*	hahreh'ts'-dah'mah
bombard, to	*hōgeki-suru*	h*oh'*ngeh-kee-soo'roo
breastwork	*kyō-heki*	kee-*oh'*-heh'kee
breech (of gun)	*hōbi*	h*oh'*bee

English.	Japanese (romanized).	Pronunciation.
breech-loader (rifle)	*kō-sō-jū*	k*oh*-s*oh*-joo
bridle	*tazuna*	tah-dzoo-nah
brigade	*ryodan*	ree-oh'dah
brigadier-general	*ryodan-chō*	ree-oh'dah-ch*oh*
bugle	*rappa*	rahp'pah
bugler	*rappa-shu*	rahp'pah-shoo
bullet (rifle)	*shōjū-dan, tama*	sh*oh'joo* dahn, tah'mah
burst, to (shell)	*haretsu suru*	hahreh'tsoo soo'roo
cable (anchor)	*ōzuna*	*oh*'dzoo-nah
camp	*jin-ya*	jeen-yah
campaign	*sen-eki*	sen-eh'kee
camping ground	*sha-ei-chi*	shah-ay-chee
cannon, gun	*tai-hō*	t*i*-h*oh*
captain (army)	*rikugun-tai-i*	reekoo'ngoon-t*i*-ee
— (navy)	*kaigun-taisa*	k*i*'-ngoon-t*i*'sah
capture, to (a ship)	*ho-kwaku suru*	hoh-k(w)ah'koo soo'roo
cartridge	*yaku-bō*	yah'koo-b*oh*
cartridge-pouch	*danyaku-bako*	dahn-yah'koo bah'koh
casualties	*shishō*	sheesh*oh'*
cavalry	*ki-hei*	kee-hay
cease fire, to	*hassha wo yameru*	hahs-shah woh yahmeh'-[roo
certificate, leave	*kyū-ka shōsho*	kee-*oo'*-kah-sh*oh'*shoh
chain, anchor-	*byōsa*	bee-*oh'*sah
change step !	*fumikae !*	foomeekah'eh !
chaplain (army)	*rikugun kwaishi*	reekoo'ngoo*n* k(w)*i*'shee
chaplain (navy)	*kaigun-kwaishi*	k*i*'ngoon-k(w)*i*'shee
charge !	*kō-geki itase !*	k*oh*-ngeh-kee eetah'seh !
chief-of-the-staff	*sambōchō*	sahm-b*oh*-ch*oh*
colonel	*taisa*	t*i*'sah
colours, the	*gun-ki*	goon-kee
column	*jutai*	joot*i'*
combatant	*sentō-in*	sent*oh'*-een
—, non-	*hi-sentō-nin*	hee-sent*oh'*-neen
command, a	*gōrei, meirei*	g*oh'*ray, may-ray'
—, to	*shirei suru*	sheeray' soo'roo
commander (navy)	*kaigun shōsa*	k*i*'ngoon sh*oh'*sah
— -in-chief	*shireichō-kwan*	sheeraych*oh'*-k(w)ahn
commanding officer	*shirei-kwan*	sheeray'k(w)ahn
commissariat	*hyō-rōtai*	hee-*oh*-r*oh'ti*
company	*chūtai*	ch*oo'ti*

English.	Japanese (romanized).	Pronunciation.
company (artillery)	*taihō-tai*	ti-hoh'-ti
—, half	*taihō han-tai*	ti-hoh' hahn-ti
compass (mariner's)	*ji-shaku*	jee-shah'koo
corporal [(press)	*gochō*	goh-choh'
correspondents	*jūgun kisha*	joo'ngoon kee'shah
court-martial	*gumpō-kwaigi*	goompoh'-kwi'nghee
crew	*nori-kumi-in*	noh'ree-koo'mee-een
cruiser	*junyō-kan*	joon-yoh'-kahn
cut (wound)	*kega kizu*	keh'ngah, kee'dsu
defaulter	*hanzaisha*	hahn-zi'shah
defaulter's drill	*shō-batsu chōren*	shoh-bah'tsoo choh'ren
defence	*bōgyo*	boh'nghee-oh
depot	*honei*	hohn-ay
deserter	*dassō-hei*	dahs-soh'-hay
detachment	*shi-tai*	shee-ti'
discipline	*gunki*	goon'kee
disembark, to	*jō-riku suru*	joh-ree'koo-soo'roo
dismount!	*geba!*	gheh'bah!
division	*shidan*	shee'dahn
doctor, the	*isha*	ee'shah
dress!	*narae!*	nah-rah'eh!
drill	*chōren, sōren*	choh'ren soh'ren
drill-book	*sōten*	soh'ten
driver	*gyosotsu*	ghee-oh-soh'tsoo
drum	*taiko*	ti'koh
drummer	*koshu*	koh'shoo
duties	*gimu*	ghee'moo
duty, guard	*shuei gimu*	shoo-ay' ghee'moo
—, outpost	*zenshō gimu*	zenshoh' ghee'moo
dynamite	*dinamito*	deenahmee'toh
embark, to	*jōsen suru*	joh-sen soo'roo
embarkation	*jōsen*	joh'sen
encampment	*yaei*	yah-ay'
enemy	*teki*	teh'kee
enemy's position	*tekijin*	teh-kee'jeen
engagement	*kas-sen*	kahs-sen
engineer (naval)	*kaigun-ki-kwan-shi*	ki'ngoon-kee-k(w)ahn-
engineers (corps)	*kōheidan*	koh'hay-dahn [shee
equipment	*gun-bi*	goon-bee
escort	*goei*	goh-ay'

English.	Japanese (romanized).	Pronunciation.
exercise, bayonet	*jūkenjutsu*	joo'kenjootsoo
expedition	*ensei*	ensay'
extend!	*chire!*	chee'reh
eyes right, dress!	*migi e, narae!*	mee'nghee eh, nah-rah'-[eh!
— left!	*hidari e!*	heedah'ree eh!
"fall in," to	*seiretsu suru*	say-reh'ts' soo'roo
farrier	*teitetsukō*	taytetsook*oh'*
fatigue (barrack)	*einai tōban*	ay-n*i'* t*oh'*bahn
field artillery	*yasen hōhei*	yah'sen h*oh'*hay
— exercises	*sōren*	s*oh*-ren
— -glass	*sōgan-kyō*	s*oh'*ngahn-kee-*oh'*
— -gun	*yahō*	yah-h*oh'*
— -hospital	*yasen byōin*	yah'sen bee-*oh'*een
— -marshal	*gensui*	ghensoo'ee
— telegraph	*yasen denshin*	yah'sen den'sheen
file (of men)	*retsu, go*	reh'tsoo, goh
fire!	*ute!*	oo'teh!
fire, to	*hassha suru, uchi-[kakeru*	hahs'shah soo'roo, oo'chee [kah-keh'roo
flag	*hata*	hah'tah
flank	*sokumen*	sohkoo'men
—, left	*hidari sokumen*	hee-dah'ree soh-koo'men
—, right	*migi sokumen*	mee'nghee soh-koo'men
fleet, the	*kantai*	kahnt*i'*
foot-soldier	*hosotsu*	hoh-soh'tsoo
forage	*kaiba, baryō*	k*i'*bah, bah-ree-*oh'*
foresight (of rifle)	*shōjaku*	sh*oh'*jah-koo
formation	*taikei*	t*i*-kay'
fortress	*hōdai, yōsai*	h*oh'*d*i*, y*oh'*s*i*
forward!	*mae e! susume!*	mah'eh eh! soo-soo'meh!
front, the	*shōmen*	sh*oh'*men
furlough	*kyūka*	kee-*oo'*kah
gallop, to	*shikku suru*	sheek'koo soo'roo
garrison	*shubihei*	shoobeehay'
general, a	*taishō*	t*i*-sh*oh'*
general officer	*shōkwān*	sh*oh'*kwahn
governor (military)	*sōtoku*	s*oh'*tohkoo
ground, parade-	*rempeiba*	rempay'bah
guard, the	*eihei*	ay-hay'
—, advanced	*zenei*	zehn-ay'
—, rear-	*kōei*	k*oh'*ay

English.	Japanese (romanized).	Pronunciation.
guard-room	*ei-sha*	ay-shah
guard, to mount	*jōban suru*	joh'bahn soo'roo
guard turn out!	*tore-jū! tachi ide!*	toh'reh-joo! tah'chee ee'-
gun, cannon	*hō*	hoh [deh!
gun-carriage	*hōshah*	hoh'shah
gunner	*hōsotsu*	hoh'soh-tsoo
gunpowder	*kwayaku*	k(w)ah-yah'koo
halt!	*tomare!*	tohmah'reh!
hay (fodder)	*magusa*	mah-ngoo'sah
head-quarters	*honei*	hohnay'
horse-brush	*umabake*	oomahbah'keh
— -cloth	*bai*	bi
— -shoe	*tettei*	tet-tay'
hospital, station-	*byōin*	bee-oh'een
hospital-ship	*byōinsen*	bee-oh'eensen
hut	*koya*	koh'yah
independent firing	*kakko shageki*	kahk'koh shah-ngeh'kee
infantry	*hohei*	hoh-hay'
—, mounted	*kiba hohei*	kee'bah hoh-hay'
inspection [ant-	*kenetsu*	kehn-eh'tsoo
instructor, assist-	*jokyō kwan*	joh-kee-oh' kwahn
insubordination	*fufuku, fuki*	foo-foo'koo, foo'kee
Intelligence Dept.	*kimitsu kyoku*	kee-mee'ts' kee-oh'koo
interpreter	*tsūyaku-kwan, tsū-ji*	tsoo'-yah'koo-kwahn,
interval	*kankaku*	kahnkah'koo [tsoo'-jee
intrench, to	*hōshō suru*	hoh-shoh soo'roo
killed in action	*senshi suru*	sen-shee soo'roo
knapsack	*hainō*	hi-noh'
ladder	*hashigo*	hah-shee'ngoh
lance, spear	*yari*	yah'ree
lancer	*sōkihei*	soh-keehay'
lashing (binding)	*kessoku*	kes-soh'koo
leave, on	*kyūka de oru*	kee-oo'kah deh oh'roo
left	*hidari*	heedah'ree
— turn	*hidari muke*	heedah'ree moo'keh
— wheel	*hidare e maware*	heedah'ree eh mahwah'-
lieutenant (army)	*chūi*	choo'ee [reh
— -colonel	*chūsa*	choo'sah
— -general	*chūjō*	choo-joh
line (rope)	*tsuna*	tsoo'nah

English.	Japanese (romanised).	Pronunciation.
line, firing	*shageki sen*	shah-ngeh'kee sen
—, in	*tsuranaru*	tsoo-rah-nah'roo
— of fire	*kwasen*	k(w)ah'sen
load, to (gun)	*hō wo sōten suru*	hoh woh soh'ten soo'roo
magazine	*kwayaku sōko*	k(w)ah-yah'koo soh'koh
— rifle	*rempatsujū*	rem-pahtsoo-joo'
main body	*hongun*	hohn'ngoon
major	*shōsa*	shoh'sah
— -general	*shōshō*	shoh'shoh
man-of-war	*gunkan*	goon'kahn
map	*dzu*	dzoo
march!	*susume!*	soosoo'meh!
—, forced	*kyōkōgun*	kee-oh-koh'ngoon
mark time, to	*ashibumi suru*	ahsheeboo'mee soo'roo
marksman	*shashu*	shah'shoo
midshipman	*kaigun-shō-i-kōhosei*	ki'ngoon-shoh-ee-koh'-
military police	*kempei*	kem-pay' [hoh-say
mine	*raikō*	ri-koh'
musketry	*shageki*	shah-ngheh'kee
— instruction	*shageki kyōren*	shah-ngheh'kee kee-oh'-
muzzle of a gun	*hōkō*	hoh-koh [ren
Navy, the	*kaigun*	ki'ngoon
officer	*shikwan, shōkō*	sh'k(w)ahn, shoh-koh
—, non-com.	*ka-shi*	kah-shee
—, petty [(N.C.O.)	*ka-shi-kwan*	kah-shee-k(w)ahn
—, staff	*sambō shōkō*	sahmboh' shoh-koh
officers' mess	*shōkō kaishokusho*	shoh'koh ki-shoh-koo-
order (command)	*meirei*	mayray' [shoh
orderly	*denrei ka-shi*	denray' kah-shee
outpost	*zenshō*	zenshoh'
parade	*kwampei shiki*	k(w)ahmpay' shee'kee
parole	*mongō*	mohngoh'
patrol	*sekikō*	seh-keekoh'
pay (officer's)	*hōkyū*	hoh-kee-oo'
— (soldier's)	*kyūryō*	kee-oo-ree-oh
paymaster	*gunri*	goon'ree
pickaxe	*tsuruppashi*	tsooroop-pah'shee
picket	*sho-hei*	shoh-hay'
pile arms!	*kume jū!*	koo'meh joo!
pontoon	*kōkyō*	koh-kee-oh

English.	Japanese (romanized).	Pronunciation.
post	*shōhsho*	sho*h*'shoh
present !	*nerae !*	neh-rah'eh !
— arms !	*sasage jū !*	sahsah'ngeh j*oo* !
prisoner of war	*fūryō*	f'ree-*oh*'
—, to take	*toriko ni suru*	tohree'koh nee soo'roo
promotion	*shinkyū*	sheenkee-*oo*'
punishment	*chō-kai*	cho*h*-ki
private, a	*heisotsu*	haysoh'tsoo
quartermaster	*kyūyō-gakari*	kee-*oo*-yo*h*-ngahkah'ree
— -sergeant	*kyūyō gunso*	kee-*oo*'yo*h* goon'soh
quarters	*ei*	ay
quick march !	*haya ashi !*	hah'yah ah'shee
range of gun	*shatei*	shah-tay'
rank (in army)	*ikai*	eek*i*'
— and file	*heishi*	hay'shee
—, front	*zenretsu*	zenreh'tsoo
—, rear	*kōretsu*	k*oh*'reh-tsoo
rations	*kōbun*	k*oh*'boon
ready !	*yōi*	y*oh*'ee
rear, the	*hai-men*	h*i*-men
rear-admiral	*kaigun-shōshō*	k*i*'ngoon-sh*oh*-sh*oh*
reconnaissance	*teisatsu*	taysah'tsoo
reconnoitre, to	*teisatsu suru*	taysah'tsoo soo'roo
recruit, a	*shimpei, nyūtaisha*	sheem-pay', nee-*oo*'t*i*-shah
Red Cross Society	*sekijūjisha*	sehkeej*oo*'jeeshah
redoubt	*kakumembō*	kah-koo-mem-b*oh*'
regiment, cavalry	*kihei rentai*	keehay' rent*i*'
—, infantry	*hohei rentai*	hoh-hay' rent*i*'
regulations	*kyōrei*	kee-*oh*'ray
reins	*tazuna*	tah-dzoo'nah
report, a	*tsūhō*	ts*oo*-h*oh*
reserves	*yobi, kōbi*	yoh'bee, k*oh*'bee
retire, retreat (to)	*taishoku suru*	t*i*-shoh'koo soo'roo
	taikyaku suru	t*i*-kee-ah'koo soo'roo
reveille	*kishōrappa*	keesh*oh*'rahppah
review	*kwampei-shiki*	k(w)ahmpay'-shee'kee
rifle	*shō-jū*	sh*oh*-joo
right, the	*migi*	mee'nghee
— turn !	*migi muke*	mee'nghee moo'keh [reh
— wheel !	*migi e maware*	mee'nghee eh mahwah'-

English.	Japanese (romanized).	Pronunciation.
roll-call, the	*tenko*	ten'koh
route-march	*kōgun*	k*oh*'ngoon
saddle	*kura*	koo'rah
sailor, bluejacket	*suihei*	soo-ee-hay'
— (merc. marine)	*suifu*	soo-ee'foo
salute, a	*keirei*	kay-ray'
—, to	*keirei suru*	kayray' soo'roo
scout, a	*saisaku*	s*i*-sah'koo
—, to	*sōsaku suru*	s*oh*'sah-koo soo'roo
sentry	*bampei*	bahm-pay'
sergeant	*gunsō*	goons*oh*'
— -major	*sōchō*	s*oh*-ch*oh*
servant, officers'	*jūsotsu*	j*oo*'sohtsoo
service (duty)	*kimmu*	keem'moo
—, special	*tokubetsu kimmu*	tohkoobeh'tsoo keem'-[moo
shell	*hōdan*	h*oh*'dahn
— fire	*hōdan shageki*	h*oh*'dahn shah-ngheh'kee
shot, a	*dangwan*	dahn'ng(w)ahn
shoulder arms!	*ninae jū!*	nee-nah'eh j*oo*!
sight (of gun)	*shōjaku*	sh*oh*'jahkoo
signal, to	*shingō suru*	sheen-g*oh*' soo'roo
signaller	*shingō-hei*	sheen-g*oh*'-hay
skirmish, to	*shōtō suru*	sh*oh*-t*oh* soo'roo
skirmishers	*sampei*	sahmpay'
skirmishing	*sansen*	sahn'sen
soldier	*heitai, gunjin*	hay-t*i*', goon'jeen
spade	*hishū*	heesh*oo*'
spy	*kanchō*	kahnch*oh*'
squadron (cavalry)	*kihei no chūtai*	keehay' noh ch*oo*t*i*'
square	*hōjin*	h*oh*'jeen
staff, the	*sambō*	sahmb*oh*'
stand at ease!	*yasume!*	yahsoo'meh!
step, pace	*hodo*	hoh'doh
stirrup	*abumi*	ahboo'mee
store, ordnance-	*hōhei bukō*	h*oh*'hay bookoh'
strategy	*senryaku*	sen-ree-ah'koo
stretcher	*tanka*	tahn'kah
— -bearer	*tankasotsu*	tahnkahsoh'tsoo
supplies, field	*senji kyūyō*	sen'jee kee-*oo*-y*oh*
supply column	*ryōshoku jūretsu*	ree-*oh*'shohkoo j*oo*'reh[tsoo

English.	Japanese (romanized).	Pronunciation.
surgeon	*guni*	goon'yee
surround, to	*gōi suru*	goh'ee soo'roo
sword	*katana, ken*	kah-tah'nah, ken
swords! carry	*sasage to!*	sahsah'ngheh toh!
tactics	*senjutsŭ*	sen-joots'
tent	*temmaku*	temmah'koo
tent-peg	*yaeikō*	yah-ay-koh'
torpedo	*suirai*	sooee-ri'
torpedo-boat	*suirai-tei*	sooee-ri'-tay
— — destroyer	*suirai kuchikutei*	sooee-ri' koocheekootay'
trenches	*zango*	zahn'ngoh
troops	*guntai*	goonti'
unfix bayonets!	*tore ken!*	toh'reh ken!
uniform	*gumpuku*	goom-poo'koo
unlimber!	*zensha wo hazuse!*	zen'shah woh hahdzoo'-seh!
veterinary surgeon	*jūi*	joo'ee
volley	*isseikwa*	ees-say'k(w)ah
volunteer, a	*shigwanhei*	shee-ngwahn'hay
wagon, a	*sha*	shah
war	*sensō, ikusa*	sensoh', ee-koo-sah
water-bottle	*suizutsu*	sooeedzoo'tsoo
wheel, to	*senkwai suru*	senk(w)i' soo'roo
who goes there?	*tare da?*	tah'reh dah?
works, earth-	*dokō*	doh-koh'
wound, a	*sōshō, kizu*	soh-shoh, kee'dzoo
wounded, the	*fushō-sha*	foo-shoh'shah

27. Cardinal Numbers. (*Gen-sūji.*)

	Japanese (rom.)*	Pronunciation.		Japanese (rom.)†	Pronunciation.
1	*ichi*	ee'chee	or	*hitotsŭ*	sheetoh'ts'
2	*ni*	nee	„	*futatsŭ*	footah'ts'
3	*san*	sahn	„	*mitsŭ*	mee'ts'
4	*shi*	shee	„	*yotsŭ*	yoh'ts'
5	*go*	goh	„	*itsŭtsŭ*	ee'ts(oo)ts'
6	*roku*	roh'koo	„	*mutsŭ*	moo'ts'
7	*shĭchi*	sh'chee	„	*nanatsŭ*	nahnah'ts'
8	*hachi*	hah'chee	„	*yatsŭ*	yah'ts'
9	*ku*	koo	„	*kokonotsŭ*	kohkohnoh'ts'
10	*jiu*	jew	„	*tō*	toh

* The words in this list are of Chinese origin. (See notes following the list.)

† These words are of purely Japanese origin.

11	*jiu-ichi** (jew-ee'chee)				
12	*jiu-ni†*	26	*ni-jiu-roku*	100	*hiaku* (hee-ah'koo)
13	*jiu-san*	27	*ni-jiu-shĭchi*	200	*ni-hiaku*
14	*jiu-shi*	28	*ni-jiu-hachi*	300	*sam-biaku*
15	*jiu-go*	29	*ni-jiu-ku*	400	*shi-hiaku*
16	*jiu-roku*	30	*san-jiu*	500	*go-hiaku*
17	*jiu-shĭchi*	31	*san-jiu-ichi*	600	*rop-piaku*
18	*jiu-hachi*	32	*san-jiu-ni*	700	*shĭchi-hiaku*
19	*jiu-ku*	40	*shi-jiu*	800	*hap-piaku*
20	*ni-jiu*	50	*go-jiu*	900	*ku-hiaku*
21	*ni-jiu-ichi*	60	*roku-jiu*	1000	*sen* (sen)
22	*ni-jiu-ni*	70	*shĭchi-jiu*	2000	*ni-sen*
23	*ni-jiu-san*	80	*hachi-jiu*	3000	*has-sen* (hahs-sen)
24	*ni-jiu-shi*	90	*ku-jiu*	10,000	*man*(mahn)
25	*ni-jiu-go*			100,000	*jiu-man* (jew-mahn)
				1,000,000	*hiaku-man*

1907 *Sen-ku-hiaku-shĭchi-nen* (sen-koo-hee-ah'koo-sh'chee-nen)

NOTES.—1. The Chinese numerals 1 to 10 must be employed only when standing *alone*, or preceding monosyllabic or uncompounded nouns derived from the *Chinese*.

2. When employed with nouns of purely Japanese origin, the terminal *tsŭ* of the Japanese numerals is dropped.

3. For further information on the use of the numerals the student is referred to Marlborough's *Japanese Grammar Self-Taught*, pp. 30-36.

28. Auxiliary Numerals.‡ (*Betsu-sŭ-ji.*)

In Japanese objects are usually enumerated as so many of a class or species, by means of "auxiliary numerals," which somewhat correspond with such an expression as "eight *head* of cattle." The following are those most commonly employed:—

Aux.	Pronunciation.	Applied to
Nin	neen ...	... human beings
hiki	hee'kee	... animals, a draught of a net, pieces of silk, etc.
wa	wah ...	... birds and bundles
hon	hohn ...	... sticks, cylinders, long and round articles (pencils, poles, masts, trees, etc.).

* The words in this list are of Chinese origin.

† Pronunciation already given in this list is not repeated.

‡ See Marlborough's *Japanese Grammar Self-Taught*, pp. 32-34.

Aux.	Pronunciation.		Applied to
mai	mi ...	...	broad flat objects (papers, plates, coins, clothing, etc.)
ken	ken ...	...	houses and buildings in general
so	soh ...	...	ships, boats, etc.
hai	hi ...	...	"fills" of a cup, bowl, glass, etc.
soku	soh'koo	...	(pairs of) shoes, socks, sandals, etc.
cho	choh ...	...	objects such as jinrikishas, palanquins
fuku	foo'koo	...	doses of medicine, "smokes" of tobacco, etc.
jo	joh ...	...	mats; it designates the areas of compartments
satsu	sah'tsoo	...	volumes of books.
suji	soo'jee	...	extended objects, as rivers, roads
dai	di ...	...	vehicles
mune	moo'neh	...	ridge-like things or houses
tsū	tsoo ...	...	letters, documents
kumi	koo'mee	...	sets of objects, as toys; companies (of persons).
tsutsumi	tsoo-tsoo'mee		packages

29. Ordinal Numbers.* (*Jo-sū-ji.*)

	Japanese (rom.)	Pronunciation.		Japanese (rom.)	
1st	*dai ichi**	di ee'chee	17th	*dai-jiu-shichi*	
2nd	– *ni*	– nee	18th	– *jiu-hachi*	
3rd	– *san*	– sahn	19th	– *jiu-ku*	
4th	– *shi*	– shee	20th	– *ni-jiu*	
5th	– *go*	– goh	21st	– *ni-jiu-ichi*	
6th	– *roku*	– roh'koo	22nd	– *ni-jiu-ni*	
7th	– *shichi*	– sh'chee'	23rd	– *ni-jiu-san*	
8th	– *hachi*	– hah'chee	24th	– *ni-jiu-shi*	
9th	– *ku*	– koo	25th	– *ni-jiu-go*	
10th	– *jiu*	– jew	26th	– *ni-jiu-roku*	
11th	– *jiu-ichi*	– jew-ee'chee	27th	– *ni-jiu-shichi*	
12th	– *jiu-ni*		28th	– *ni-jiu-hachi*	
13th	– *jiu-san*		29th	– *ni-jiu-ku*	
14th	– *jiu-shi*		30th	– *san-jiu*	
15th	– *jiu-go*		40th	– *shi-jiu*	[koo
16th	– *jiu-roku*		100th	– *hiaku*	hee'ah'-

* Instead of employing "dai" *before*, "ban" (bahn) may be used *after* the cardinals. See *Japanese Grammar Self-Taught*, p. 34.

30. Collective and Fractional Numbers, etc.

(Shu-gō-sū, bun-sū, nado.)

English.	Japanese (romanized).	Pronunciation.
All	*mina* (emphatic,	mee'nah, meen'nah
century, a	*isseiki* [*minna*)	ees-say'kee
half-a-century	*hanseiki*	hahn-say'kee
couple (pair)	*ittsui*	eet-tsoo'ee
double (twice)	*bai, baihodo, nijiu*	bi, bi-hoh'doh, nee'jew
dozen	*ichi daasu*	ee'chee d*ah*'soo
half-a-dozen	*han-daasu*	hahn-d*ah*'soo
eighth	*hachi-bu-no-ichi*	hah'chee-boo-noh-ee'chee
first time	*hajime-ni*	hah-jee'meh-nee
fourth, a	*shi-bu-no-ichi*	shee-boo-noh-ee'chee
gross, a	*jiu-ni-daasu, ichi gorosu*	jew-nee-d*ah*'soo, ee'chee-gohroh'soo
half, a	*hambun*	hahm'boon
once	*ichi do*	ee'chee doh
part (portion), a	*bubun*	boo'boon
quarter (¼)	*shi-bu-no-ichi, ni-bu-go-rin*	shee'boo-noh-ee'chee, nee-boo-goh-reen
score	*ni-jiu*	nee-jew
second time	*ni-do-me*	nee-doh-meh
single (only one)	*tatta hitotsū no*	taht'tah sh'toh'tsoo noh
third, a	*sam-bu-no-ichi*	sahm-boo-noh-ee'chee
third time, the	*san-do-me*	sahn-doh-meh
three-fold	*san-bai-no*	sahn-bi'-noh
three-quarters (¾)	*shi-bu-no-san*	shee-boo-noh-sahn
twice	*ni-do*	nee-doh
— as much	*ni-bai*	nee-b*i* [ree
the whole, all the	*mina de, sokkuri*	mee'nah deh, sohk-koo-

31. Adjectives.* (*Kei-ō-shi.*)

Able	*dekiru*	dehkee'roo
afraid	*kowai*	koh-wi' [nah
all	*nokorazu, mina*	nohkohrah'dzoo, mee'-
alone	*hitori de*	sh'toh'ree deh
amusing	*omoshiroi*	ohmoh-shee-roy' [ts'
another	*hoka no, mō hitotsū*	hoh'kah noh, m*oh* sh'toh'-
awkward	*heta, buchō hō*	heh'tah, boo-ch*oh*' h*oh*
bad	*warui*	wahroo'ee

* For Grammatical Notes see Marlborough's *Japanese Grammar S.T.*, pp. 61-66.

English.	Japanese (romanized).	Pronunciation.
beautiful	*kirei (na), utsŭku-*	keeray' (nah), oots'koo-
big	*ōkii, ōki (na) [shii*	*oh'*kee, *oh'*kee(nah) [sh*ee'*
bitter	*nigai*	nee-nghi'
blind	*mekura (no)*	meh-koo'rah (noh)
both	*ryō-hō, dore mo*	ree-*oh*-h*oh*, doh'reh moh
broad	*hiroi*	hee-roy'
bulky	*kasabatta*	kahsahbaht'tah
busy	*isogashii*	eesoh-ngah-sh*ee'*
certain	*tashĭka (na)*	tah-sh'kah (nah)
cheap	*yasui*	yahsoo'ee
clean	*kirei (na)*	kee-ray' (nah)
clever	*jōzu (na), rikō (na)*	j*oh'*dzoo (nah), reek*oh'*
cold (weather)	*samui*	sahmoo'ee [(nah)
— (to the touch, or hands, feet, &c.)	*tsumetai*	tsoomeh-t*i'*
common (ordinary)	*nami no*	nah'mee noh
convenient	*benri na*	ben'ree nah
cool	*suzushii*	soodzoosh*ee'*
damp	*shimeppoi*	sheemep-poy'
dangerous	*kennon (na), abunai*	ken'nohn (nah), ahboon*i'*
dark	*kurai*	koo-r*i'*
deaf	*tsumbō (no)*	tsoomb*oh'* (noh)
dear (expensive)	*takai*	tahk*i'*
deep	*fŭkai*	f(oo)k*i'* [noh
different	*chigatta, betsu (no)*	chee-ngaht'tah, beh'tsoo
difficult	*muzukashii [shii*	moodzookahsh*ee'* [sh*ee'*
dirty	*kitanai, kitanara-*	keetahn*i'*, keetahnahrah-
distant	*empō (na), tōi*	emp*oh'* (nah), t*oh'*ee
dull (weather)	*kumotta, uttōshii*	koomoht'tah, oot-t*oh'*sh*ee*
early	*hayai*	hah-y*i'*
easy	*yasashii, zōsa nai*	yah-sah-sh*ee'*, z*oh'*sah n*i*
empty	*kara (na)*	kah'rah (nah)
even (smooth)	*taira (na) [(no)*	t*i'*rah (nah) [(noh)
false	*hontō de nai, uso*	hohnt*oh'* deh n*i*, oo'soh
far	*tōi, empō (na)*	t*oh'*ee, emp*oh'* (nah)
fast (speedy)	*hayai*	hah-y*i'*
fine (minute)	*komakai*	kohmahk*i'*
— (beautiful, &c.)	*kirei na, rippa na*	keeray' nah, reep'pah nah
flat	*taira (na), hirattai*	t*i'*rah (nah), heeraht-t*i'*
fond (very)	*dai sŭki*	d*i* s'kee

English.	Japanese (romanized).	Pronunciation.
foolish	*bakarashii*	bah-kahrahshee'
foreign	*seiyō no, gwaikoku*	say-yoh' noh, gwi-koh'koo
free	*jiyū (na)* [(*no*)	jee-yoo' (nah) [(noh)
fresh (eggs, &c.)	*umi-tate*	oo'mee-tah'teh
— (cool)	*suzushii*	soodzooshee'
full	*ippai (na)*	eep-pi' (nah) [shee'
funny	*omoshiroi, okashii*	ohmohsheeroy', ohkah-
general(customary)	*ippan no, futsū no*	eep'pahn noh, foo-tsoo'
glad	*ureshii*	ooreh-shee' [noh
good	*yoi, yoroshii*	yoy, yohrohshee'
grand (splendid)	*rippa (na), migoto*	reep'pah (nah), mee-
hard (solid)	*katai* [(*na*)	kah-ti' [ngoh'toh (nah)
— (difficult)	*mudzukashii*	moodzookahshee'
healthy	*tassha na*	tahs'shah nah
heavy	*omoi, omotai*	ohmoy', ohmohti'
high	*takai*	tah-ki'
honest	*shōjiki (na)*	shoh'jeekee (nah)
hot	*atsui, attakai*	ahtsoo'ee, aht-tah-ki'
— (as mustard)	*karai*	kahri'
idle	*nora-kurana,* *namaketa*	noh'rah-koo-rah'nah, nah-mah-keh'tah
ignorant	*mugaku na*	moo-ngah'koo nah
ignorant of	*fu-annai*	foo-ahn-ni'
ill (sick) [sequence	*byōki*	bee-oh'kee
important, of con-	*daiji na*	di'jee nah
impossible	*dekinai*	deh-keeni'
inconvenient, un-	*fu-benri na*	foo-ben'ree nah
incorrect [suitable	*machigatta*	mah-chee-ngaht'tah
interesting	*omoshiroi*	ohmoh-sheeroy'
just (equitable)	*tadashii, kōhei na*	tahdahshee', koh'hay nah
kind	*shinsetsu (na)*	sheenseh'tsoo (nah)
lame	*chimba, bikko*	cheem'bah, beek'koh
large, great	*dai* (in compounds),	di, oh-kee
late	*osoi* [*ōkii*	oh-soy'
lazy	*bushō (na)*	booshoh' (nah)
left (-hand)	*hidari*	heedah'ree
light (in weight)	*karui*	kahroo'ee
— (not dark)	*akarui*	ahkahroo'ee
little (small)	*chiisa (na), chiisai*	chee'sah (nah), cheesi'
long	*nagai*	nah-nghi'

English.	Japanese (romanized).	Pronunciation.
loose	*yurui*	yooroo'ee
loud	*takai ōki* (*na*)	tahki, *oh*'kee (nah)
low	*hĭkui*	h(ee)koo'ee
many	*ōku no, ōi*	*oh*'koo noh, *oh*'ee
middle	*mannaka*	mahn-nah'kah
more	*motto*	moht'toh
much	*takŭsan*	tah-k'sahn'
narrow	*semai*	seh-m*i*'
near	*chikai*	cheek*i*'
necessary	*kanjin na, hitsuyō na*	kahn-jeen nah, heetsoo-*yoh*' nah
next	*tsugi no*	tsoong'ee noh
numerous	*ōi*	*oh*'ee
old (of things)	*furui*	fooroo'ee
— (of persons)	*toshiyori* (*no*), *toshitotta*	tohshee-yoh'ree (noh), toh-shee-toht'tah
opposite	*no mukō ni*	noh mook*oh*' nee
other	*betsŭ no, hoka no*	bets' noh, hoh'kah noh
painful	*itai*	eet*i*'
pale	*ao-zameta*	ah'oh-zahmeh'tah
polite	*teinei* (*na*)	tay-nay' (nah)
poor	*bimbō* (*na*)	beemb*oh*' (nah)
pretty	*kirei* (*na*), *utsukushii*	keeray' (nah), ootsookoo-sh*ee*'
proper	*sōtō* (*na*), *sōō* (*na*)	s*oh*-t*oh* (nah), s*oh*-*oh* (nah)
pure (unadulterated)	*junsui na*	joonsoo'ee (nah)
queer	*myō* (*na*), *kitai* (*na*)	mee-*oh*' (nah), keet*i*' (nah)
quick	*hayai*	hah-y*i*'
quiet	*shizuka* (*na*)	sheedzoo'kah (nah)
rare	*mare* (*na*)	mah'reh (nah)
raw (uncooked)	*nama* (*no*)	nah'mah (noh)
real	*hontō* (*no*), *makoto* (*no*)	hohnt*oh*' (noh), mahkoh'-toh (noh)
rich	*kane-mochi* (*no*)	kah'neh moh'chee (noh)
right (proper)	*honto* (*no*), *ii*	hohn'toh (noh), *ee*
— (-hand)	*migi*	mee'nghee
ripe (of fruit)	*juku shĭta*	joo'koo sh'tah'
rough	*arai*	ahr*i*'
round	*marui*	mahroo'ee
rude	*shitsurei* (*na*), *shikkei* (*na*)	sheetsooray' (nah), sheek-kay' (nah)
safe	*daijobu* (*na*)	d*i*-j*oh*'boo (nah)

English.	Japanese (romanized).	Pronunciation.
same	*onaji*	ohnah'jee
shallow	*asai*	ahsi'
short (in length)	*mijikai*	meejeeki'
silly	*baka (na)*	bah'kah (nah)
simple	*wakari-yasui, tegarui*	wahkah'ree-yahsoo'ee, teh-ngahroo'ee
sleepy	*nemui*	neh-moo'ee
slovenly	*zon-zai na*	zohn-zi nah
slow	*osoi*	oh-soy'
small	*chiisai, chiisa (na)*	cheesi', chee'sah (nah)
soft	*yawarakai, yawa-*	yahwahrahki', yahwah-
solid	*katai* [*raka (na)*	kahti' [rah'kah (nah)
sorry (for another)	*kinodoku*	keenohdoh'koo
sour	*suppai*	soop-pi'
special	*betsudan na, tokubetsu na*	betsoo'dahn nah, toh-koo-behtsoo nah
square	*shĭkaku (na)*	sh'kah'koo (nah)
stiff	*katai*	kahti'
still (tranquil)	*shizuka (na)*	sheedzoo'kah (nah)
straight	*massugu (na)*	mahs-soo'ngoo (nah)
strange	*fūshigi (na)*	f(oo)shee'nghee (nah)
strong	*tsuyoi*	tsoo-yoy' [(nah)
stupid	*baka(na), tomma(na)*	bah'kah (nah), tohm-mah
sweet	*amai*	ahmi'
tall	*sei no takai*	say noh tahki'
that	*sono*	soh'noh
thick (consistency)	*koi*	koy
— (in dimension)	*atsui*	ahtsoo'ee
tight	*katai*	kahti'
troublesome	*urusai, mendō (na)*	ooroosi', mendoh' (nah)
true	*honto (no), makoto (no)*	hohn'toh (noh), mahkoh'-toh (noh)
unavoidable	*yondokoronai* [*(na)*	yohndohkohrohni' [(nah)
uncomfortable	*kyū kutsū, fujiyū*	keeoo-koots', foojee-yoo'
unhappy	*fu-shiawase (na)*	foo-sheeahwah'seh (nah)
unkind	*funinjō, fūshinsetsu (na)* [*fu-kwai*	fooneenjoh, foo'sheenset-soo (nah) [foo-ki
unwell	*ambai ga warui,*	ahmbi' gah wahroo'ee,
urgent	*kyū na* [*tatsu*	kee-oo' nah [nee tah'tsoo
useful	*chōhō (na), yaku ni*	choh-hoh (nah), yah'koo

English.	(romanized).	Pronunciation.
useless	*yaku ni tatanai*	yah'koo nee tahtahni'
usual	*tsūrei (no), heizei (no)*	tsoo'ray (noh), hay-zay' (noh)
— (suitable)	*atarimae no, tekitō na*	ahtahreemah'eh noh, teh-kee-toh' nah
vain	*nama-iki (na), kōman (na)*	nah'mah-ee'kee (nah) koh'mahn (nah)
various	*iro-iro (na), ironna*	ee'roh-ee'roh (nah), ee-rohn'nah
warm	*atatakai, atataka (na), attakai*	ahtahtahki', ahtahtah'-kah (nah), attahki'
weak	*yowai*	yoh-wi'
well (in health)	*jōbu (na), tassha (na)*	joh'boo (nah), tahs'shah (nah)
whole	*mina, sōtai (no)*	mee'nah, soh'ti (noh)
wide	*hiroi*	heeroy'
worth (in value)	*atai, ne-uchi*	ahti', neh-oo'chee
worthless	*tsumaranai, yaku-nashi*	tsoomahrahni', yahkoo-nah'shee
wrong	*warui, machi-gatta*	wahroo'ee mah'chee-ngaht'tah
young	*wakai*	wahki'

32. Verbs.* (*Dōshi.*)

To accept	*uketoru*	ookehtoh'roo
to add	*kuwaeru, awaseru*	koowah'ehroo, ahwahseh'-roo
to admit (allow to enter)	*ireru*	eereh'roo
to allow	*yurusu*	yooroo'soo
to answer	*hentō suru, kotaeru*	hentoh' soo'roo, kohtah'-eh-roo
to arrange (put in order)	*kata wo tsukeru, soroeru*	kah'tah woh tsookeh'roo, sohroh'ehroo
to arrive	*tōchaku suru, tsuku*	toh'chahkoo soo'roo, tsoo'koo
to ask	*kiku, tou*	kee'koo, toh'oo
to assist	*tetsudau*	teh-tsoodow'
to bark	*hoeru*	hoh-eh'roo
to bathe	*mizu wo abiru*	mee'dzoo woh ahbee'roo
to beat	*butsu, utsu*	boo'tsoo, oo'tsoo
to become	*naru*	nah'roo
to begin (*intr.*)	*hajimaru*	hahjeemah'roo
to believe	*shinjiru*	sheen-jee'roo
to bend (*intr.*)	*magaru*	mah-ngah'roo

* See Marlborough's *Japanese Grammar Self-Taught*, pp. 39-61.

English.	Japanese (romanized).	Pronunciation.
to bite	*kui-tsŭku, kamu*	koo'ee-ts'koo, kah'moo
to boil water (*tr.*)	*wakasu*	wahkah'soo
to boil (*intr.*)	*waku*	wah'koo
to borrow	*kariru*	kahree'roo
to break (*trans.*)	*kowasu, oru*	kohwah'soo, oh'roo
to break (*intr.*)	*kowareru, oreru*	kohwahreh'roo, ohreh'-
to bring (an object)	*motte kuru*	moht'teh koo'roo [roo
— (a person)	*tsurete kuru*	tsooreh'teh koo'roo
to build	*tateru*	tahteh'roo
to buy	*kau*	kow
to call (waken)	*okosu*	ohkoh'soo
to carry	*hakobu*	hahkoh'boo
to change (*trans.*)	*kaeru, torikaeru*	kah'ehroo, tohreekah'-
— (*intr.*)	*kawaru*	kahwah'roo [ehroo
to choose	*erabu*	ehrah'boo
to clear (weather)	*agaru*	ah-ngah'roo
to climb	*noboru*	nohboh'roo
to collect (*trans.*)	*yoseru*	yohseh'roo
— (*intr.*)	*atsumeru*	ah-tsoo-meh'roo
to come	*kuru*	koo'roo
to come in	*hairu*	hi'roo
to consent	*shōchi suru*	sh*oh'*chee soo'roo
to cough	*seki ga deru*	seh'kee gah deh'roo
to count	*kazoeru*	kahzoh'eh-roo
to cry, weep	*naku*	nah'koo
to cut	*kiru*	kee'roo
to dance	*odoru*	ohdoh'roo [roo
to decide	*kimeru, kettei suru*	keemeh'roo, ket-tay' soo'-
to die	*shinu, shinuru*	shee'noo, sheenoo'roo
to dislike	*kirau*	kee-row' (like *now*)
to dismiss	*hima wo yaru*	hee'mah woh yah'roo [soo
to do	*suru, nasu, itasu*	soo'roo, nah'soo, eetah'-
to doubt	*fŭshin ni omoŭ*	f'sheen' nee ohmoh'(oo)
to dream	*yume wo miru*	yoo'meh woh mee'roo
to drink	*nomu*	noh'moo [soo
to dry (*trans.*)	*kawakasu, hosu*	kah-wah-kah'soo, hoh'-
to eat	*taberu* [polite)	tahbeh'roo [(oo')
to engage	*tanomŭ* (*yatoŭ*, less	tahnoh'm(oo) [yahtoh-
to explain, make clear	*bemmei suru, toki akasu*	bem-may'soo'roo, toh'kee ahkah'soo

English.	Japanese (romanized).	Pronunciation.
to fail	*sokonau, hazureru*	soh-koh-now', hahdzoo-reh'roo
to faint	*me wo mawasu, kizetzu suru*	meh woh mahwah'soo, keezeh'tzoo soo'roo
to fall	*ochiru*	oh-chee'roo [roo
to feel	*kanjiru, oboeru*	kahnjee'roo, ohboh'eh-
to fill	*ippai ni suru*	eep-p*i*' nee soo'roo
to find	*mi-ataru, mi-dasu, mi-tsŭkeru*	mee-ahtah'roo, mee-dah'-soo, mee-ts(oo)keh'roo
to finish	*shimau*	sheemow' (like *cow*)
to fish	*uwo wo tsuru*	oo'woh woh tsoo'roo
to fly	*tobu*	toh'boo
to follow	*tsuite iku*	tsooee'teh ee'koo
to forget	*wasureru*	wah-sooreh'roo
to forgive	*yurusu*	yooroo'soo
to gain	*mōkeru*	m*oh*'kehroo
to gather (*tr.*)	*atsŭmeru*	ahts'meh'roo
to get in	*hairu*	h*i*'roo
to get out	*deru*	deh'roo
to get up (rise)	*okiru*	ohkee'roo
to give	*yaru*	yah'roo
to go	*iku*	ee'koo
to go away	*itte shimau*	eet'teh sheemow'
to go in	*hairu*	h*i*'roo
to go out	*deru*	deh'roo
to guide	*annai suru*	ahn-n*i*' soo'roo
to hang (*tr.*)	*tsuru, kakeru, tsuri-ageru*	tsoo'roo, kahkeh'roo, tsoo'ree-ah-ngheh'roo
to have	*motsu, motte iru*	moh'tsoo, moht'teh ee'-
to hear	*kiku*	kee'koo [roo
to help	*sewa wo suru, tetsu-*	seh'wah woh soo'roo, teh-
to hire (a servant)	*yatoŭ* [*dau*	yahtoh'(oo) [tsoodow'
to hire(a house,etc.)	*kariru*	kahree'roo
to hit	*butsu, ateru*	boo'tsoo, ah-teh'roo
to hold (contain)	*hairu*	h*i*'roo
to be hungry	*haraga heru, o naka ga suki*	hahrah'ngah heh'roo, oh nah'kah gah soo'kee
to hurt (*intr.*)	*itamu* [*masŭ*	eetah'moo [mah's'
to hurt one's-self	*kega wo suru*	keh'ngah woh soo'roo
to interfere	*jama suru*	jah'mah soo'roo

English.	Japanese (romanized).	Pronunciation.
to interpret	*tsŭben wo suru*	tsoo'ben woh soo'roo
to invite	*maneku*	mahneh'koo
to join (*trans.*)	*tsugu, awaseru*	tsoo'ngoo, ahwahseh'roo
to keep (things)	*tamotsu, motte iru*	tahmoh'tsoo, moht'teh
to kill	*korosu*	kohroh'soo [ee'roo
to knock	*tataku*	tahtah'koo
to know	*shiru, shitte iru*	shee'roo, sheet'teh ee'roo
to label	*fuda wo tsukeru*	foo'dah woh tsookeh'roo
to last	*motsu*	moh'tsoo
to laugh	*warau*	wah-rah'oo
to lead	*hĭku, annai suru*	h(ee)koo, ahn-nĭ' soo'roo
to learn	*manabu, narau*	mahnah'boo, nahrah'oo
to leave off (cease)	*yosu, yameru*	yoh'soo, yahmeh'roo
to lend	*kasu*	kah'soo
to let (permit)	*saseru, yurusu*	sahseh'roo, yooroo'soo
to lie down	*neru*	neh'roo
to lift	*mochi-ageru*	moh'chee-ah-ngheh'roo
to light (a fire)	*hi wo taku*	hee woh tah'koo [roo
to light (a lamp)	*rampu wo tsŭkeru*	rahm'poo woh ts(oo)keh'-
to like	*konomu, sŭki*	kohnoh'moo, s'kee'
to live (reside)	*sumau*	soomow'
to lock	*jō wo orosu*	*joh* woh ohroh'soo
to look at	*miru*	mee'roo
to look for	*sagasu*	sah-ngah'soo [now'
to lose (*tr.*)	*naku suru, ushinau*	nah'koo soo'roo, oosheeo-
to love	*aisuru*	*i*-soo'roo [koo'roo
to make	*koshiraeru, tsukuru*	koh-sheerah'ehroo, tsoo-
to make a mistake	*ayamatsu*	ah-yah-mah'tsoo
to manage	*tori-atsŭkau*	toh'ree-ah-ts'kow'
to mend	*naosu, tsŭkuroŭ*	nah-oh'soo, ts'kooroh'-
to mix (*trans.*)	*mazeru*	mahzeh'roo [(oo)
to move (*trans.*)	*ugokasu*	oo-ngohkah'soo
to move (*intr.*)	*ugoku*	oo-ngoh'koo
to object	*koshō wo iŭ*	kohsh*oh'* woh ee*oo'*
to observe	*mi-ukeru, ki-ga*	mee-ookeh'roo, kee-ngah
	tsŭku	ts(oo)koo' [roo
to offer	*ageru, susumeru*	ah-ngeh'roo, soosoomeh'-
to omit	*otosu*	ohtoh'soo
to open (*trans.*)	*akeru*	ahkeh'roo
to open (*intr.*)	*aku*	ah'koo

English.	Japanese (romanized).	Pronunciation.
to order (at shop)	*atsuraeru*	ahtsoorah'ehroo
to order (command)	*ii-tsŭkeru*	*ee*-ts(oo)keh'roo
to pack	*ni zukuri wo suru*	nee dzookoo'ree woh soo'roo
to pay	*harau*	hahrow'
to permit	*shōchi suru*	sh*oh*'chee soo'roo
to perspire	*ase ni naru*	ah'seh nee nah'roo
to pick	*tsumu*	tsoo'moo
to pick up	*hiroŭ*	heeroh'(oo)
to play	*asobu*	ahsoh'boo
to pour	*tsugu*	tsoo'ngoo
to prepare	*koshiraeru, shĭtaku wo suru*	kosheerah'ehroo, sh'tah'koo woh soo'roo
to prevent	*jama wo suru, samatageru*	jah'mah woh soo'roo, sahmahtah-ngeh'roo
to promise	*yakŭsoku suru*	yah-k(oo)soh'koo soo'roo
to pull	*hĭku*	h(ee)koo
to push	*osu*	oh'soo
to put	*oku, sueru*	oh'koo, soo-eh'roo
to put off	*nobasu*	nohbah'soo
to put on (don)	*kiru*	kee'roo
to rain	*ame ga furu*	ahmeh gah foo'roo
to raise	*ageru*	ah-ngheh'roo
to read	*yomu*	yoh'moo
to receive	*uke-toru*	oo'keh-toh'roo
to recommend	*susumeru*	soosoomeh'roo
to refuse	*kotowaru*	kohtohwah'roo
to remain	*nokoru, amaru*	nohkoh'roo, ahmah'roo
to remember	*oboeru*	ohboh'ehroo
to repay	*kaesu, henkyaku suru*	kah'eh-soo, hen-kee-ah'koo soo'roo
to rest	*yasumu*	yahsoo'moo
to return (*trans.*)	*kaesu*	kah'eh-soo
to return (*intr.*)	*kaeru*	kah'eh-roo
to ride	*noru*	noh'roo
to ring (*intr.*)	*narasu*	nahrah'soo
to ring (*trans.*)	*naru*	nah'roo
to roast	*yaku*	yah'koo
to rub	*kosuru*	koh-soo'roo
to run	*kakeru*	kahkeh'roo
to save	*tasŭkeru*	tah-s'keh'roo

English.	Japanese (romanized).	Pronunciation.
to say	*hanasu, iu*	hahnah'soo, ee'oo
to see	*miru*	mee'roo
to seem, appear	*mieru*	mee-eh'roo
to send	*yaru, tsŭkawasu*	yah'roo, ts(oo)kahwah'soo
to sew	*nuu*	noo
to share	*wakeru, bumpai suru*	wahkeh'roo boompi' soo'roo
to shave	*hige wo suru (soru)*	hee'ngheh woh soo'roo (soh'roo)
to shine	*teru*	teh'roo
to show	*miseru*	meeseh'roo
to shut (*trans.*)	*shimeru*	sheemeh'roo
to sing (of persons)	*utau;* (birds, *naku*)	ootow' (nah'koo)
to sit (as European)	*koshi wo kakeru*	koh'shee woh kahkeh'roo
to sit (as Japanese)	*suwaru*	soowah'roo
to sleep	*neru*	neh'roo
to smoke	*tabako wo nomu*	tahbah'koh woh noh'moo
to sneeze	*kŭshami wo suru*	k'shah'mee woh soo'roo
to sow	*maku*	mah'koo
to spend	*tsuiyasu, tsŭkau*	tsoo-ee-yah'soo, ts'kow'
to spoil	*sonjiru*	sohn-jee'roo
to stand (*intr.*)	*tatsu*	tah'tsoo
to start (set out)	*shuttatsu suru, tatsu*	shoot-tah'tsoo soo'roo, tah'tsoo
to steal	*nusumu*	noosoo'moo
to stop (*trans.*)	*tomeru*	tohmeh'roo
to stop (*intr.*)	*tomaru*	tohmah'roo
to sweep	*haku*	hah'koo
to swim	*oyogu*	oh-yoh'ngoo
to take	*toru*	toh'roo
to take care	*ki wo tsŭkeru*	kee woh ts(oo)keh'roo
to talk	*hanasu*	hahnah'soo
to tear (*trans.*)	*saku, yabuku*	sah'koo, yahboo'koo
to tell	*hanasu, iu*	hahnah'soo, ee'oo
to tell (relate)	*kataru*	kahtah'roo
to thank	*rei wo iu*	ray woh ee'oo
to think	*omou, zonjiru*	ohmoh'(oo), zohn-jee'roo
to throw	*nageru, hōru*	nah-ngheh'roo, hoh'roo
to tie	*shibaru*	sheebah'roo
to touch	*sawaru, fureru*	sahwah'roo, foo-reh'roo
to travel	*ryokō suru, tabi wo suru*	ree-ohkoh' soo'roo, tah'-bee woh soo'roo
to try	*yatte miru, tamesu*	yaht'teh mee'roo, tah-meh'soo

English.	Japanese (romanized).	Pronunciation.
to turn (*trans.*)	*mawasu*	mahwah'soo
to turn (*intr.*)	*mawaru*	mahwah'roo
to understand	*wakaru*	wahkah'roo
to use	*mochiiru, tsukau*	moh-chee'roo, tsookow'
to wait	*matsu*	mah'tsoo
to walk	*aruku*	ahroo'koo [moo
to want	*iru, hoshii, nozomu*	ee'roo, hoh-shee, nohzoh'-
to warn	*imashimeru, kotowaru*	eemah-sheemeh'roo, koh-toh-wah'roo
to waste (*trans.*)	*tsuiyasu, muda ni tsŭkau*	tsoo-ee-yah'soo, moo'dah nee ts(oo)kow'
to watch, to keep watch	*ban wo suru*	bahn woh soo'roo
to wear (*trans.*)	*kiru*	kee'roo
to wear (*intr.*)	*motsu*	moh'tsoo
to weigh (*trans.*)	*hakaru*	hahkah'roo
to wipe	*nugū fŭku*	noo-ngoo' f(oo)koo'
to wish	*nozomu, hoshii* (adj.)	noh-zoh'moo, hoh-shee'
to work	*hataraku*	hahtahrah'koo
to wrap up	*tsutsumu*	tsoo-tsoo'moo
to yawn	*akubi suru*	ahkoo'bee soo'roo

33. Adverbs, Particles, Conjunctions, Pronouns,* &c.

(Fukushi, Teniwoha, Setsuzokushi, Daimeishi.)

English	Japanese	Pronunciation
about (nearly)	*oyoso, kurai (gurai),*	ohyoh'soh, koori' (goori'),
above	*no ue* [*hodo*	noh oo'eh [hoh'doh
according to	*ni yotte*	nee yoht'teh
across	*yoko ni*	yoh'koh nee
after	*no nochi ni*	noh noh'chee nee
afterwards	*nochi ni*	noh'chee nee
again	*mata*	mah'tah
ago	*mae ni*	mah'eh nee
almost	*hotondo*	hohtohn'doh [nee
already	*mohaya, sude ni*	moh-hah'yah, soo'deh
also	*mo, yahari, yappari*	moh, yah-hah'ree, yahp-
always	*itsudemo*	eetsoodeh'moh [pah'ree
among	*no uchi ni*	noh oo'chee nee
anybody	*dare de mo*	dah'reh deh moh

* For the grammar of these Parts of Speech see Marlborough's *Japanese Grammar Self-Taught.*

English.	Japanese (romanized).	Pronunciation.
anything	*nan de mo*	nahn deh moh
any time	*nan doki de mo, itsu de mo*	nahn doh'kee deh moh, ee'tsoo deh moh
anywhere	*doko de mo*	doh'koh deh moh
around	*no mawari ni*	noh mahwah'ree nee
at	*ni, de*	nee, deh
at last	*yōyaku, tsui ni*	yo*h*'yahkoo, tsoo'ee nee
because	*kara*	kah'rah
before	*saki, no mae ni*	sah'kee, noh mah'eh nee
behind	*no ura ni, no ushiro ni*	noh oo'rah nee, noh ooshee'roh nee
below	*shĭta*	sh'tah'
beneath	*no shĭta ni*	noh sh'tah nee
besides	*no hoka ni*	noh hoh'kah nee
between	*no aida ni*	noh *i*'dah nee
by	*ni, de, no soba ni*	nee, deh, noh sohbah nee
certainly (without doubt)	*chigai nai, mochiron*	chee-ngh*i*' n*i*, mohchee'rohn
daily	*mainichi*	m*i*-nee'chee
down	*shĭta (ye)*	sh'tah (yeh)
downstairs	*shĭta ni*	sh'tah nee
early	*hayai*	hah-y*i*'
especially	*betsu ni, koto ni*	beh'tsoo nee, koh'toh nee
even	*sura, sae, de mo*	soo'rah, sah'eh, deh moh
everywhere	*doko de mo, hōbō*	doh'koh deh moh, h*oh*'b*oh*
except	*no hoka ni*	noh hoh'kah nee
far	*tōi, empō (na)*	t*oh*'ee, emp*oh* (nah)
from	*yori, kara*	yoh'ree, kah'rah
here	*koko, kochi (ra)*	koh'koh, koh'chee (rah)
how?	*ikaga? dō? do shĭte?*	eekah'ngah? d*oh*? doh sh'teh?
how long?	*itsu made?*	ee'tsoo mah'deh?
how many?	*ikutsu?*	eekoo'tsoo?
how often?	*iku tabi? iku do?*	ee'koo tah'bee? ee'koo doh?
immediately	*sassoku, sugu ni*	sahs-soh'koo, soo'ngoo nee
in	*ni*	nee
inside	*ni, no naka ni*	nee, noh nah'kah nee
into	*ni, no naka ye*	nee, noh nah'kah yeh
just (exactly)	*chōdo*	ch*oh*'doh
nearly	*mo sŭkoshi de*	moh s'koh'shee deh
next	*tsugi ni*	tsoo'nghee nee

English.	Japanese (romanized).	Pronunciation.
notwithstanding	*ni kamawazu, ni kakawarazu*	nee kahmahwah'dzoo, nee kahkahwahrah'dzoo
of	*no*	noh [chee'rohn
of course	*moto yori, mochiron*	moh'toh yoh'ree, moh-
often	*tabi-tabi*	tah'bee-tah'bee
only	*tada, bakari*	tah'dah, bahkah'ree
over	*no ue ni*	noh oo'eh nee
probably	*ōkata, tabun*	*oh*'kah-tah, tah'boon
quietly	*shizuka ni*	sheedzoo'kah nee
rather (somewhat)	*iku bun ka*	ee'koo boon kah
recently	*konaida*	kohn*i*'dah
seldom (with neg.	*metta ni*	meht'tah nee
separately [verb)	*wakete, betsu (ni)*	wah-keh'teh, beh'tsoo
slowly	*shidzuka ni*	sheedzoo'kah nee [(nee)
somebody	*dare ka*	dah'reh kah
something	*nani ka*	nah'nee kah [foo'shee
sometimes	*toki doki, ori-fushi*	toh'kee doh'kee, oh'ree
somewhere	*doko ka, dokka*	doh'koh kah, dohk'kah
soon	*jiki ni, hodo naku*	jee'kee nee, hoh'doh nah'-
still (yet)	*nao, mada*	nah'oh, mah'dah [koo
than	*yori*	yoh'ree
then	*sono toki*	soh'noh toh'kee
there	*asŭko, soko, achira* [politer)	ah's'koh, soh'koh, ah-chee'rah [kah'rah
therefore	*da kara. (desu kara*	dah kah'rah, deh'soo
through	*tōshite, tōtte*	t*oh*'sh'teh, t*oh*t'teh
till	*made*	mah'deh
to	*ni, ye*	nee, yeh
too (too much)	*amari*	ahmah'ree
too (as well)	*mo, yahari*	moh, yah-hah'ree
towards	*no hō ye*	noh *hoh* yeh
under	*no shita ni*	noh sh'tah' nee
unfortunately	*ai-niku*	*i*-nee'koo
upon	*no ue ni*	noh oo'eh nee
usually, generally	*atarimae, taigai*	ahtahreemah'eh, *ti*-ngh*i*'
when?	*itsu?*	ee'tsoo?
where?	*doko?*	doh'koh?
where	*no tokoro*	noh tohkoh'roh [keh deh
why?	*naze? dō iu wake de?*	nah'zeh? d*oh* ee'oo wah'-
with (together)	*to issho ni*	toh ees'shoh nee

CONVERSATIONAL PHRASES AND SENTENCES.

NOTE.—(1) The Japanese equivalents are not in all cases literal translations, but are those which the same set of circumstances would draw from Japanese speakers.

(2) In social intercourse with the Japanese it should be borne in mind that they are perhaps the most sensitive nation in the world; e.g., a mere hint of displeasure will be taken deeply to heart and remembered—seldom, however, with any feeling of malice.

Useful & Necessary Idiomatic Expressions & Phrases.*

(Hitsu yō no gengo, hōgen, tō.)

English.	Japanese (romanized).	Pronunciation.
Good morning!	*O hayō!*	oh hah-*yoh'*!
Good day; *or*, How do you do?	*Konnichi wa!*	kohnnee'chee wah!
Good evening! (meeting)	*Komban wa!*	kohm'bahn wah!
Good night! (to one going to bed)	*O yasumi nasai!*	oh yahsoo'mee nahs*i'*!
Excuse me; *or*, I beg your pardon	*Go men nasai*	goh men nahsi'
Oh, don't mention it!	*Dō itashimashĭte!*	do*h* eetahsheemah'sh'teh!
Thank you	*Arigato*	ahree-ngah'toh
No, thank you	*Arigato, Yoshimashō*	ahree-ngah'toh, yoh-sheemah-sh*oh'*
Thank you very much for your assistance	*Ōki ni o sewa sama ni narimashĭta*	*oh'*kee nee oh seh'wah sah'mah nee nahreemah'sh'tah
Thanks for your trouble	*Go kurō sama*	goh koor*oh'* sah'mah
I apologise for interrupting you	*O jama itashimashĭta*	oh jah'mah eetahsheemah'sh'tah
It does not matter	*Chitto mo kamaimasen*	cheet'toh moh kahm*i*mah'sen
I can scarcely ask (asking a favour)	*Mōshi-kane masŭ-ga*	m*oh'*shee-kah'neh mah's'ngah

* For the rules of Japanese Grammar, including Syntax, see Marlborough's *Japanese Grammar Self-Taught.*

English.	Japanese (romanized).	Pronunciation.
Please do, I beg	*Dōka o negai mōshimasŭ*	doh'kah oh neh-nghi' moh'sheemahs'
You are quite (indeed) welcome	*Yō koso oide na sai mashĭta*	yoh koh'soh oy'deh nah-si'mah'sh'tah [s'
Just as you please	*Go katte shidai desŭ*	goh kaht'teh sheedi' deh'-
You are quite right	*Go mottomo de gozaimasŭ*	goh moht-toh'moh deh goh-zi-mah's'
Do as you please	*Go katte ni nasai*	goh kaht'teh nee nahsi'
Take as much as you please	*O iriyō dake o tori nasai*	oh ee-ree-yoh' dah'keh oh toh'ree nahsi'
It is lucky that...	*Yoi ambai ni...*	yoy ahmbi'nee...
As you know...	*Go zonji no tori*	goh zohn'jee noh toh'ree
It must be done	*Shinakŭcha naran koto desŭ*	sheenah'k'chah nah'rahn koh'toh deh's'
What are you doing? (*to* inferior)	*Nani wo suru?*	nah'nee woh soo'roo? [mah's'?
— (*to* equal *or* sup.)	*Nani wo nasaimasŭ*	nah'nee woh nahsi-
Please come back soon	*Mata o hayaku o kaeri nasaimashi* [*nasai*	mah'tah oh hah-yah'koo oh kah-eh'ree nahsi-mah'shee [nahsi'
Come here	*Kochira ye oide*	koh-chee'rah yeh oy'deh
I have come on business [come?	*Yō ga atte mairimashĭta*	yoh gah aht'teh mi-ree-mah'sh'tah [kah?
When will you	*Itsŭ oide nasaru ka?*	ee'ts' oy'deh nahsah'roo
Will you come?	*Oide nasaimasŭ ka?*	oy'deh nahsi-mah's' kah?
Where are you going?	*Dochira ye o ide de gozaimasŭ?*	dohchee'rah yeh oh ee'-deh deh goh-zimah's'?
Go and look	*Itte goran nasai*	eet'teh goh'rahn nahsi'
What is the matter? *or*, What is it?	*Nanda?* (fam.) *Dō shimashĭta!*	nahn'dah? doh shee-mah'sh'tah? [yah'koo
As soon as possible	*Naru-take hayaku*	nah'roo-tah'keh hah-
Oh no! that is not	*Sō ja gozaimasen*	soh jah goh-zi-mah'sen
If possible [so	*Narō koto nara*	nahroh' koh'toh nah'rah
I don't quite understand	*Hakkiri to wakarimasen*	hahk-kee'ree toh wah-kahreemah'sen
I haven't the slightest idea [mean?	*Mattaku zonjimasen* [*desŭ?*	maht-tah'koo zohnjee-mah'sen [keh deh's'?
What does this	*Kore wa dō iŭ wake*	kohreh wah doh eeoo wah-
I don't know	*Zonjimasen* [*n' desŭ*	zohnjeemah'sen [n'deh's'
I have never seen it	*Mita koto ga nai*	mee'tah koh'toh gah ni

English.	Japanese (romanized).	Pronunciation.
I haven't seen you for a long time	*Shibaraku o me ni kakarimasen*	sheebahrah'koo oh meh nee kah-kahreemah'sen
What do you say?	*Nani wo osshaimasŭ*	nahnee woh ohs-shimah's'
Who said so? [about it	*Dare ga sō iimashĭta?*	dah'reh gah soh eemah'-sh'tah? [shoh'
I will speak to him	*Danjite mimashō*	dahnjee'teh meemah-
He won't hear of it [on	*Naka-naka shōchi shimasen*	nah'kah-nah'kah shoh'-chee sheemah'sen
He cannot be relied	*Ate ni narimasen*	ahteh nee nahreemah'sen
He is honest and hard-working	*Ano hĭto wa, shōjiki de, yoku hatarakimasŭ*	ah'noh sh'toh' wah, shoh'jeekee deh, yoh'koo hah-tahrahkeemah's'
You must not do that	*Sō shĭcha ikemasen* [*masen*	soh sh'chah' eekehmah'-sen [eekehmah'sen
Don't tell anyone	*Hĭto ni itt'chya ike-*	sh'toh nee eet-t' ch(ee)ah
I will do my best	*Narutake hone-otte yarimashō*	nahrootah'keh hoh'neh-oht'teh yahreemah-shoh'
I can do without it	*Nakute mo ii n' desŭ* [(familiar)	nahkoo'teh moh ee n' deh's' [shee
It will do afterwards	*Ato demo yoroshii*	ah'toh deh'moh yohroh-
It will do at your leisure	*Go tsugō no toki de yoroshiu gozaimasŭ*	goh tsoo-ngoh' noh toh'-kee deh yohrohshee'oo goh-zi-mah's'
Be careful!	*Ki wo tsukero!*	kee woh tsookeh'roh!
I will bring it for you	*Motte kite agemashō*	moht' teh kee'teh ah-ngeh-mah-shoh'
Do you want this?	*Kore wa o iriyō desŭ ka?* [*raitai*	koh'reh wah oh ee'ree-yoh' deh's' kah? [mohri-ti
I want an answer	*Henji wo shite mo-*	hen'joo woh shee'teh
Wait a moment [answer?	*Sukoshi mate* (fam.); *Sukoshi omachi nasai* (polite)	sookoh'shee mah'teh; sookoh'shee oh-mah'-chee nah-si' [ngah?
What is your	*O henji wa ikaga?*	oh hen'jee wah eekah'-
Do you like this?	*Kore wo o suki desŭ*	koh'reh woh oh soo'kee
I like it very much	*Dai sŭki desŭ* [*ka?*	di s'kee deh's' [deh's'kah?
How do you like it?	*Ikaga desŭ?*	eekah'ngah deh's'?
Kindly let me know at once	*Dōzo sugu ni kikashĭte kudasai*	doh-zoh soo'ngoo nee kee-kah'sh'teh koodahsi'
You are very fortunate	*O shiawase de gozaimasŭ*	oh shee-ahwah'seh deh goh-zi-mah's'

English.	Japanese (romanized).	Pronunciation.
You need not be anxious	*Go shimpai ni wa oyobimasenŭ*	goh sheempi' nee wah oh-yohbeemahseh'n'
It is too difficult	*Amari mutsukashii n' desŭ*	ahmah'ree mootsookah'-shee n'deh's' [tah
It is well done	*Yoku deki mashĭta*	yoh'koo deh-kee mah'sh'-
What is your address?	*Go jū sho wa dochira desŭ*	goh *joo* shoh wah doh-chee'rah deh's'?
My address is...	*Watakŭshi no tokorogaki wa ... de gozaimasŭ*	wahtah'k'shee noh toh-koh'roh-ngah'kee wah ... deh goh-zi-mah's
This is my address	*Watakŭshi no jūsho wa koko desŭ*	wahtah'k'shee noh *joo'*-shoh wah koh'koh deh's'
Give me his address	*Ano hĭto no tokorogaki wo kudasai*	ah'noh sh'toh noh toh-koh'roh-ngah'kee woh koodahs*i'* [mah's'
He lives in Hiogo	*Hiōgo ni orimasŭ*	hee*oh*'ngoh nee obree-
He resides at Tokyo [suppose so)	*Tōkyō ni sunde orimasŭ*	t*oh*-k(ee)y*oh* nee soon'-deh ohreemah's'
So it seems. (Yes, I	*Sō da sō desŭ*	s*oh* dah s*oh* deh's'
Do you speak English?	*Anata Igirisu kotoba wo go zonji desŭ ka?*	ahnah'tah ee-nghee-ree'-soo kohtoh'bah woh goh zohn'jee deh's' kah?
I am English	*Watakŭshi wa Igirisu desŭ*	wahtah'k'shee wah ee-nghee-ree'soo deh's'
I don't understand	*Wakarimasen*	wahkahreemah'sen
I can speak a little Japanese	*Watakŭshi Nihon-go wa sukoshi dekimasŭ*	wahtah'k'shee nee'hohn-ngoh wah sookoh'shee dehkeemah's'
I had not time	*Hima ga nakatta n' desŭ*	hee'mah gah nahkaht'-tah n'deh's' [mah'sen
I really cannot wait	*Matcha oraremasen*	maht'chah ohrahreh-
As you see	*Goran no tōri*	goh'rahn noh t*oh*'ree
Where were you seen?	*Doko de miraremashĭta ka?*	doh'koh deh meerahreh-mah'sh'tah kah?
Is it convenient to-morrow?	*Miōnichi tsugō wa yoroshii n' desu ka?*	mee*oh*'neechee tsoo-ng*oh*' wah yohrohsh*ee*' n' deh's' kah?
I will return it to-morrow	*Miōnichi o kayeshi mōshimasŭ*	mee*oh*'neechee oh kah-yeh'shee m*oh*sheemah's'
Just as you like	*Go katte shidai desŭ*	goh kaht'teh sheed*i*'deh's'

English.	Japanese (romanized).	Pronunciation.
Please let me know immediately	*Sugu ni kikashite kudasai*	soo'ngoo nee keekah'-sh'teh koodahsi'
He has already left	*Mō o kayeri ni narimashĭta*	moh oh kah-yeh'ree nee nahreemah'sh'tah
[not know		
He probably does	*Shiranai n'deshō*	sheerahni' n'deh'shoh
This article wears well	*Kono shina wa mochi-ga yoroshii n' desŭ*	koh'noh shee'nah wah moh'chee-ngah yoh-rohshee' n'deh's'
Are there any book-shops in Ōsaka?	*Ōzaka ni honya ga gozaimasŭ ka?*	ohzah'kah nee hohn'yah gah goh-zi-mah's' kah?
To be sure there are!	*Arimasŭ to mo!*	ahreemah's' toh moh!
I enquired, but there was none	*Tadzunemashĭta keredomo, gozaimasenŭ deshĭta*	tahdzoonehmah'sh'tah keh-rehdoh'moh, goh-zi-mah-seh'n' deh'sh'tah
I see you for the first time	*Hajimete o me ni kakarimasŭ*	hahjeemeh'teh oh meh nee kahkahreemah's'
Where are you going?	*Dochira ye o ide de gozaimasŭ?*	doh-chee'rah yeh oh ee'-deh deh goh-zi-mah's'?
Come here; I have something for you to do	*Yō ga aru kara, kochi o ide* (fam.)	yoh gah ah'roo kah'rah, koh'chee oh ee'deh
May I ask who you are, sir?	*Donata de irasshai-masŭ ka?*	dohnah'tah deh eerahs-shi-mah's' kah?
When do you return to Europe?	*Itsu Yōroppa ye o kaeri ni narimasu ka?*	ee'tsoo yoh'rohp-pah yeh oh kaheh'ree nee nah-ree-mah's' kah?
Is anything the matter with you?	*Dō ka nasaimashĭta ka?* [*shĭta?*	doh kah nahsi-mah'sh'tah kah? [sh'tah?
Who said so?	*Dare ga sō iima*	dah'reh gah soh eemah'-
Be pleased to wait	*O machi nasai*	oh mah'chee nah-si'
Go and wait at the school, please	*Gakkō ye itte o machi nasai*	gahk-koh' yeh eet'teh oh mah'chee nahsi' [shi'
You come as well	*Anata mo irrasshai*	ahnah'tah moh eer-rahs-
I am told he returned yesterday	*Sakujitsu kayerimashĭta sō desŭ*	sahkoojee'tsoo kah-yeh-reemah'sh'tah soh deh's'
You must be careful	*Yōjin shinai to ikemasen-zo!*	yoh'jeen sheeni' toh ee-kehmah'sen-zoh!
I did not break it; *i.e.*, it was not I who broke it	*Kowashĭta no wa watakŭshi de gozaimasenŭ*	kohwah'sh'tah noh wah wah-tah'k'shee deh goh-zi-mahseh'n'

English.	Japanese (romanized.)	Pronunciation.
That is the important point	*Soko ga kanjin desŭ*	soh'koh gah kahn'jeen deh's'
Why?	*Naze desŭ?* (fam.)	nah'zeh deh's'?
In that case it is all right	*Sonnara yoroshiu gozaimasŭ*	sohn-nah'rah yohroh-shee'oo goh-zi-mah's'
It is extremely inconvenient	*Goku goku tsugō ga warui*	goh'koo goh'koo tsoo-ngoh' gah wahroo'ee
There is no help for it	*Shĭ-kata-ga nai*	sh'-kah'tah-ngah ni
Under what circumstances?	*Dō iu shidai de?*	doh ee'oo sheedi' deh?
What is the reason?	*Dō iu wake desŭ?*	doh ee'oo wah'keh deh's'?
What is the matter?	*Dō shĭta no desŭ?*	doh sh'tah noh deh's'?
There is no mistake about it!	*Sore ni sōi nai n' desŭ!*	soh'reh nee soh'ee ni n' deh's'!
You were certainly to blame	*Omaye wa warui no ni chigai nai*	ohmah'yeh wah wahroo'-ee noh nee chee-nghi ni
What is your opinion?	*Anata wa dō iu o kangae desŭ?*	ahnah'tah wah doh ee'oo oh kahn-ngah'eh deh's'?
Please make a note of it	*Dōka a kaki-tome wo negaimasŭ*	doh'kah oh kah-kee-toh'-meh woh neh-nghimahs'
I say! Mr....	*Moshi, ... San!*	moh'shee! ... sahn!
Look!	*Goran nasai!*	goh'rahn nahsi!
It is indeed grand	*Makoto ni o rippa de gozaimasŭ*	mahkoh'toh nee oh reep'-pah deh goh-zi-mah's'
Without ceremony	*Go yenrio naku*	goh yenree'oh nah'koo
Speak louder, please	*Motto ō-goe de osshatte kudasaimashi*	moht'toh oh-ngoh'eh deh ohs-shaht'teh koodah-si-mah'shee
Is it not beautiful?	*Rippa na mono ja nai ka?*	reep'pah nah moh'noh jah ni kah?

Expressions of Emotion.* (*Kantō shi.*)

English.	Japanese (romanized.)	Pronunciation.
Indeed! (Is that so?)	*Sō desŭ ka?*	soh deh's' kah?
How can you say such a thing!	*Sonna koto wo osshatte!*	sohn'nah koh'toh woh ohs-shaht'teh!
It is a pity that...	*Oshii koto ni wa ...*	oh-shee' koh'toh nee wah...
I am sorry for you	*O kinodoku sama*	oh keenohdoh'koo sah'-mah
I see!	*Naruhodo!*	nahroohoh'doh!
Excuse me for having inconvenienced you†	*Kore wa, o jama wo itashimashĭta*	koh'reh wah, oh jah'mah woh eetahsheemah'-sh'tah

* See Note 2, page 72.

† On concluding a visit.

English.	Japanese (romanized).	Pronunciation.
What ! (protest)	*Nani !*	nah'nee ! [neh !
What a pity !	*Oshii koto desŭ, ne !*	oh-shee' koh'toh deh's',
I feel ashamed	*Memboku ga gozaimasen*	memboh'koo gah goh-zi-mah'sen [deh's'
It is a nuisance	*Komatta koto desŭ*	kohmaht'tah koh'toh
It *was* jolly !	*Taihen ni omoshirō gozaimashĭta !*	ti'hen nee ohmohsheeroh' goh-zi-mah'sh'tah !
I am very glad of it	*Makoto ni yorokobashiū gozaimasŭ* [*masŭ*	mahkoh'toh nee yohrohkohbahshee-oo' goh-zi-mah's' [beemah's'
I am delighted	*Hijō ni yorokobi-*	heejoh' nee yohrohkoh-
I am glad	*Sore wa ureshiū gozaimasŭ*	sohreh wah ooreh-sheeoo' gohzimah's' [mah's'
I congratulate you	*O medetō zonjimasŭ*	oh meh-dehtoh' zohnjee-
Don't talk nonsense ! [noise !	*Baka iu-na !*	bah'kah ee'oo-nah !
Don't make such a	*Yakamashii !*	yahkahmahshee' !
Don't bother !	*Urusai !*	ooroosi' ! [dah !
It is most annoying !	*Komatta mono da !*	kohmaht'tah moh'noh
I don't care !	*Kamai ya shinai !*	kahmi' yah sheeni' ! [ni' !
This won't do !	*Kore de wa ikenai !*	koh'reh deh wah eekeh-
I should never think of saying such a thing !	*Sonna koto wa, ii ya itashimasen !*	sohn'nah koh'toh wah, ee yah eetahsheemah'-sen !
—of doing such a thing !	*Sonna koto wa shi ya shimasen*	sohn'nah koh'toh wah shee yah sheemah'sen !
It is none of your business	*Omae no kamatta-koto ja nai*	ohmah'eh noh kahmaht'-tah koh'toh jah ni
You had better hold your tongue	*Damatte iru hō ga ii !*	dahmaht'teh ee'roo hoh gah ee !
Do as I order you !	*Watakŭshi no iu tōri ni itase !*	wahtah'k'shee noh ee'oo toh'ree nee eetah'seh !
You have my strict orders	*Kataku ii-tsuketa zo*	kahtah'koo ee-tsookeh'tah zoh
Why don't you go when I tell you ?	*Ikettara ikanai ka ?* (familiar)	eeket-tah'rah eekahni' kah ?
Get away, *or* Be off !	*Achi ike !*	ah'chee ee'keh !
Get out of the way and let me pass !	*Waki e yore !*	wah'kee eh yoh'reh !
Insolent fellow !	*Atsŭkamashii !*	ahts'kahmahshee' !

Enquiries. (*Ukagau Koto.*)

NOTE.—In asking for information, it is usual to preface any enquiry with the formula "*Go men nasai!*" (Excuse me). European gentlemen raise the hat at the same time, whether the query be addressed to a male or a female. The formula used in thanking a stranger for information received is "*Kore wa, domō! arigatō sonjimasu!*"—the nearest English equivalent to which is "Thanks very much."

English.	Japanese (romanized).	Pronunciation.
What is the Japanese name for this?	*Kono mono wa, Nihon-go de nan to moshimasŭ?*	koh'noh moh'noh wah, nee'hohn-goh deh nahn toh moh-sh'mah's'?
What is this made of?	*Kore wa, nan de dekite orimasŭ!*	koh'reh wah, nahn deh deh-kee'teh ohreemah's'
What is this thing?	*Kono mono wa, nanda?*	koh'noh moh'noh wah, nahn'dah?
What ought I to do?	*Dō itashitara yokarō?*	doh eetah-sh'tah'rah yohkahroh'?
What is this for?	*Kore wa, nan' ni tsukaimasŭ?*	koh'reh wah, nah'n' nee tsooki-mah's'?
What is he doing?	*Naniwo shite imasŭ?*	nah'nee woh sh'teh' eemah's'?
What have you come for?	*Nani shi ni kita?* (in anger)	nah'nee shee nee kee'-tah?
What could have been the reason?	*Dō iu wake de gozaimashitarō?*	doh ee'oo wah'keh deh goh-zi-mah'sh'tahroh'?
What is it all about?	*Dō shita mon' desŭ!*	doh sh'tah moh'n' deh's'?
What do you propose to do to him?	*Dō nasaimasŭ? Dō nasaru otsumori desŭ?*	doh nahsi-mah's'? doh nahsah'roo ohtsoo-moh'ree deh's'?
What has happened	*Dō shimashita?*	doh sheemah'sh'tah?
What is your name?	*O namaye wa nan' to osshaimasŭ?*	oh nahmah'yeh wah nah'n' toh ohshi-mah's'?
My name is Smith	*Watakŭshi wa Smith to mōshimasŭ*	wahtah'k'shee wah smith toh mohsh'mah's'
What time does the lecture begin tomorrow?	*Miōnichi no enzetsu wa, nan-ji kara hajimarimasŭ?*	meeoh'neechee noh en-zeh'tsoo wah, nahn-jee kah'rah hahjeemahreemah's'?
You had better enquire	*Kiite miru ga ii*	kee'teh mee'roo gah ee
Please enquire for me (on my behalf)	*Kiite itadakitō gozaimasŭ*	kee'teh eetahdahkeetoh' goh-zi-mah's'
I will enquire for you	*Kiite agemashō*	kee'teh ah-ngeh-mah-shoh'

English.	Japanese (romanized).	Pronunciation.
What salary should I pay per month?	*Hito-tsŭki no shirei wa, dono kurai yattara yokarō?*	sh'toh'-ts'kee' noh sheeray' wah, doh'noh koor*i* yaht-tah'rah yohkahr*oh'*
Oh! I should say... would be sufficient	*Ma! ... de jūbun de gozaimashō*	mah! ...deh j*oo*boon' deh goh-zi-mahsh*oh'*
What age are you?	*O toshi wa o ikutsu ni o nari nasaru?*	oh toh'shee wah oh eekoo'tsoo nee oh nah'ree nahsah'roo?
Which is the shortest way to...?	*...ye iku ni wa, dore ga chika-michi desŭ ka?*	...yeh ee'koo nee wah, doh'reh gah chee'kahmee'chee deh's' kah?
Is this the way to...?	*...ye wa kore de yoi no desŭ ka?*	...yeh wah koh'reh deh yoy noh deh's' kah?
How far is it to...?	*...ye dono kurai arimasŭ ka?*	...yeh doh'noh koor*i'* ahreemah's' kah?
How far is it from here?	*Koko kara dono kurai hanarete imasŭ?*	koh'koh kah'rah doh'noh koor*i'* hahnahreh'teh eemah's?
Where is the police station?	*Keisatsu-sho wa dochira de gozaimasŭ?*	kaysah'tsoo-shoh wah doh-chee'rah deh goh-*zi*-mah's'?
Does Mr. ... live in this street?	*Kono machi ni ... to mōsu hito ga gozaimasŭ ka?*	koh'noh mah'chee nee... toh m*oh'*soo sh'toh gah goh-z*i*-mah's' kah?
Can you direct me to his house?	*Ano hito no uchi wo oshiete kudasaimasen ka?*	ah'noh sh'toh noh oo'chee woh oh-shee-eh'teh koodahs*i*-mah'sen kah?
Where does he live?	*Doko ni sunde orimasŭ ka?*	doh'koh nee soon'deh ohreemah's' kah?
Can I see Mr. ...?	*...San ni o me ni kakaritō gozaimasŭ?*	...sahn nee oh meh nee kahkahreet*oh'* goh-*zi*-mah's'?
On making enquiries...	*Kiite mita tokoro* [*ga...*	kee'teh mee'tah tohkoh' [roh gah ...
When do you return to your country?	*Itsu o kuni ye o kaeri nasaimasŭ ka?*	ee'tsoo oh koo'nee yeh oh kah-eh'ree nahs*i*mah's' kah?
Isn't it finished yet?	*Mada dekite imasen* [*ka?*	mah'dah deh-kee'teh ee- [mah'sen kah?
Is it convenient today?	*Konnichi tsugō wa yoroshiū gozaimasŭ ka?*	kohn-nee'chee tsoo-ng*oh'* wah yohrohshee-*oo'* goh-*zi*-mah's' kah?

Travelling: By Railway. *(Ryo-kō: Kishade.)*

(For Vocabulary see page 35.)

English.	Japanese (romanized).	Pronunciation.
Order a carriage to take me to the station	*Suteishon ye iku kara basha wo tanonde o-kure*	sootay'shohn yeh ee'koo kah'rah bah'shah woh tahnohn'deh oh-koo'reh
To the station, quick!	*Suteishon ye hayaku*	sootay'shohn yeh hah-yah'koo
Hurry up!	*Hayaku! hayaku!*	hah-yah'koo! hah-yah'-koo!
Shall I be in time?	*Mada ma ni aima-shō ka?*	mah'dah mah nee *i*-mah-sh*oh'* kah?
Let us go	*Ikō ja nai ka?* (fam.)	eek*oh'* jah n*i* kah?
I think I shall go	*Ikō ka to omoimasŭ*	eek*oh'* kah toh oh-moh'-ee-mah's'
The first train in the morning	*Ichi-ban kisha*	ee'chee-bahn kee'shah
I shall set off to-morrow	*Miōnichi shuttatsu shimasŭ*	meeo*h'*neechee shoot-tah'tsoo sheemah's'
There is plenty of time	*Mada yohoda aida ga arimasŭ*	mah'dah yoh-hoh'doh *i'*-dah gah ahreemah's'
Is the luggage ready?	*Nimotsŭ no shitaku wa ii ka?*	neemoh'ts' noh sheetah'-koo wah *ee* kah?
Please help me with my luggage	*Kono nimotsŭ wo chotto tetsu-datte kudasai*	koh'noh neemoh'ts' woh choht'toh tetsoodaht'-teh koodahs*i'*
Which is your luggage?	*Dore ga anata no nimotsŭ desŭ ka?*	dohreh gah ahnahtah noh neemoh'ts' deh's' kah?
Will you take charge of my luggage?	*Nimotsŭ wo o adzu kari kudasaru ka?*	neemoh'ts' woh oh ah-dzookah'ree koodah-sah'roo kah?
Take care!	*Ki wo tsŭkete kuda-sai!*	kee woh ts'keh'teh koo-dahs*i'*!
Are you sure you have forgotten nothing?	*Wasure-mono wa nai ka?*	wahsoo'reh-moh'noh wah n*i'* kah?
I will go and get a ticket	*Kippu wo katte kimashō*	keep'poo woh kaht'teh keemahsh*oh'*
Where is the booking-office?	*Kippu no uridokoro wa doko ni ari-masŭ ka?*	keep'poo noh ooreedoh-koh'roh wah doh'koh nee ahreemah's' kah?
Give me a first-class return to Tokio	*Dōka Tōkyō made no jōtō ōfŭku-gippu wo ichi-mai kudasai*	d*oh'*kah t*oh*-kee-*oh* mah'-deh noh j*oh-toh oh'*-f'koo-gheep'poo woh ee'chee-m*i* koodahs*i'*

English.	Japanese (romanized).	Pronunciation.
I want return tickets	*Ōfŭku gippu wo kudasai*	oh'f'koo gheep'poo woh koodahsi'
1st class; 2nd; 3rd	*Jōtō; chūtō; katō*	joh-toh; choo-toh; kahtoh'
Where are you going, sir?	*Dochira ye irasshaimasŭ?*	doh-chee'rah yeh eerahs-shi-mah's'?
I am going through [to...	*...made mairimasŭ*	...mah'deh mi-reemah's'
All right, come along	*Sa! o tomo itashimashō*	sah! oh toh'moh eetahsheemahshoh'
What is the fare?	*Chinsen wa ikura?*	cheen'sen wah eekoo'rah?
How much is the excess? (on luggage)	*Yo-bun no chin-sen wa ikura desŭ ka?*	yoh-boon noh cheen-sen wah eekoo'rah deh's' kah?
When is the next train for...?	*... made, tsugi no kisha wa nan-ji ni demasŭ ka?*	... mah'deh, tsoo'nghee noh kee'shah wah nahn-jee nee dehmah's' kah?
Is this the train for...?	*Kore wa ... yuki no kisha desŭ ka?*	koh'reh wah......yoo'kee noh kee'shah deh's' kah?
What time is there a train for...?	*... ye yuku kisha wa nan-ji ni demasŭ ka?*	...yeh yoo'koo kee'shah wah nahn-jee nee deh-mah's' kah?
When will the train [start?	*Ressha wa itsu de-* [*masŭ ka?*	res'shah wah ee'tsoo deh- [mah's' kah?
At once, sir	*Tadaima*	tahdi'mah
Is there a non-smoking carriage?	*Tabako wo kinjite aru kyakusha ga aru ka?*	tahbah'koh woh keenjee'-teh ah'roo kee-ah-koo'-shah gah ah'roo kah?
Where is your ticket, please?	*Kippu wo chotto haiken?*	keep'poo woh choht'toh hi'ken?
Is this an express?	*Kore wa kyukō-ressha desŭ ka?*	koh'reh wah kee-ookoh'-res'shah deh's' kah?
Am I in the right train for...?	*Kono notte iru kisha wa...made yuku ni chigai wa arimasen ka?*	koh'noh noht'teh ee'roo kee'shah wah...mah'deh yoo'koo nee chee-nghi' wah ahreemah'sen kah?
Where do I change for...?	*...made yuku ni wa, doko de nori-kae shimasu ka?*	...mah'deh yoo'koo nee wah, doh'koh deh noh'-ree-kah'eh sheemah'-soo kah?
There! the train is [starting	*Sora! kisha ga* [*deru*	soh'rah! kee'shah gah [deh'roo
That seat is engaged	*Sono tokoro wa fusayatte imasŭ*	soh'noh tohkoh'roh wah foosahngaht'teh eemah's'

English.	Japanese (romanized).	Pronunciation.
Do I change here for...?	*...ye yuku ni wa koko de nori-kaemasŭ ka ?*	...yeh yoo'koo nee wah koh'koh deh noh'ree-kah-eh-mah's' kah ?
This is not a smoking carriage	*Kono kyakusha de wa tabako wo nomu koto ga kinjite imasŭ*	koh'noh kee-ahkoo'shah deh wah tahbah'koh woh noh'moo koh'toh gah keenjee'teh eemah's'
Do you object to smoking ?	*Tabako wo nonde mo anata ni wa sashitsukae ga gozaimasen ka ?*	tahbah'koh woh nohn'deh moh ahnah'tah nee wah sah-shee-tsookah'eh gah goh-*zi*-mah'sen kah ?
May I open (close) the window ?	*Mado wo akete (shimete) mo yō gozaimasŭ ka ?*	mah'doh woh ahkeh'teh (sheemeh'teh) moh y*oh* goh-*zi*-mah's' kah ?
Do we stop long here ?	*Kono tei-sha-ba ni nagaku tomarimasŭ ka ?*	koh'noh tay-shah-bah nee nah-ngah'koo toh-mahreemah's' kah ?
Show these ladies to the waiting room	*Kono fujin gata wo kiusokujo ye go annai mōshi-te kudasai*	koh'noh foo'jeen gah'tah woh kew-soh-koo'joh yeh goh ahn-n*i*' mo*h*'-shee-teh koodahs*i*'
Lavatory	*Benjo. Chōzuba*	ben'joh ; ch*oh*'dzoobah
Which is the way out ?	*De-guchi wa doko desŭ ka ?*	deh-goo'chee wah doh'-koh deh's' kah ?
There is the way out	*De-guchi wa asŭko de yozaimasŭ*	deh-goo'chee wah ah's'-koh deh goh-*zi*-mah's'
I have come to meet you, sir	*Danna ! o mukai in mairimashĭta*	dahn'nah ! oh mook*i*' nee m*i*-reemah'sh'tah

By Road : Hiring Conveyances.

(*Ōrai de : Kuruma wo yatou koto.*)

(See Vocabulary 21, page 35.)

Order a 'riksha [man !	*Jinrikisha wo tanonde kudasai*	jeenree'keeshah woh tah-nohn'deh koodahs*i*'
Here ! jinrikisha-	*Oi ! kuruma-ya !*	oy ! kooroo'mah-yah !
Here ! bring a double 'riksha	*Oi ! ni-nin-nori no kuruma it-chō motte koi*	oy ! nee-neen-noh'ree noh kooroo'mah eet-ch*oh*' moht'teh koy
[horses	*[basha*	[bah'shah
A carriage with two	*Ni-hiki dachi no*	nee-hee'kee dah'chee noh

English.	Japanese (romanized).	Pronunciation.
Here! bring one 'riksha	*Oi! jinrikisha it-cho motte koi*	oy! jeenree'keeshah eet-choh moht'teh koy
A 'riksha drawn by one man (two men)	*Ichi-nim-biki (ni-nim-biki) no kuruma*	ee'chee-neem-bee'kee (nee-neem-bee'kee) noh kooroo'mah
A 'riksha to seat one person (two persons)	*Ichi-nin-nori (ni-nin-nori) no kuruma*	ee'chee-neen-noh'ree (nee-neen-noh'ree) noh kooroo'mah
How much to take me to Tokio?	*Tōkyō made dono-kurai de noseru ka?*	to*h*kee-*oh* mah'deh doh'-noh-koor*i*' deh nohseh'-roo kah?
How many are there in your party?	*O iku-tari de gozai-masŭ?*	oh ee'koo-tah'ree deh goh-*zi*-mah's'?
There are four of us	*Yottari desŭ*	yoht-tah'ree deh's'
Take me to the station	*Suteishon made no-sete yatte kure*	sootayshohn mahdeh noh-seh'teh yaht'teh koo'reh
All right, please step in	*He! Yoroshiū gozai-masŭ O meshi na-saimashi*	heh! yohrohshee*oo*' goh-*z*imah's' oh meh'shee nahs*i*-mah'shee
Will he be able to [go?	*Ikareru d' arō ka?*	eekahreh'roo d'ahr*oh*' [kah?
Put up the hood	*Horo wo agete kure*	hoh'roh woh ah-ngheh'-teh koo'reh
Lower the hood	*Horo wo totte kure*	hoh'roh woh toht'teh [koo'reh
Stop here a moment	*Koko de sukoshi matte o kure*	koh'koh deh soo-koh-shee maht'teh oh koo'reh
Let me get out here	*Koko de oroshite o-kure*	koh'koh deh ohroh'sh'teh oh-koo'reh
How far is it to...?	*...made donogurai [aru?*	...mah'deh dohnoh-ngoo-[r*i*' ahroo?
Which is the road to...?	*...ye iku michi wa, dochira de goz-aimasŭ?*	...yeh ee'koo mee'chee wah, doh-chee'rah deh goh-*zi*-mah's'?
How is the road ahead?	*Kore kara saki no michi wa, dō desŭ?*	kohrehkahrah sahkee noh meechee wah, d*oh* deh's'?
Please tell me the way	*Michi wo oshiete kudasai*	mee'chee woh oh-shee-eh'teh koodahs*i*'
Will it be possible to go?	*Iku koto-ga deki-mashō ka?*	ee'koo koh'toh-ngah deh-keemahsh*oh*' kah?
Your horse is ready, sir	*Danna, o ŭma no shĭtaku wa yoro-shiū gozaimasŭ*	dahn'nah, oh'm-mah'noh sh'tah'koo wah yohroh-shee-*oo*' gohz*i*mah's'

English.	Japanese (romanized).	Pronunciation.
It is no distance on to the next place	*Koko kara saki wa, jiki desŭ*	koh'koh kah'rah sah'kee wah, jee'kee deh's'?
How many *ri* is it from here?	*Kore yori nan'ri hodo aru?*	koh'reh yoh'ree nahn'ree hoh'doh ah'roo?
How dreadfully bad the road is!	*Osoroshii dōmo michi ga warui*	ohsohrohsh*ee'* d*oh*'moh mee'chee gah wahroo'ee
How many *ri* is it to the next town?	*Tsugi no shŭku made nan ri gozaimasŭ?*	tsoo-nghee' noh sh'koo' mah'deh nahn ree goh-zimah's'?
[on?	[*desŭ ka?*	[n'deh's' kah?
Must I go straight	*Massugu ni iku n'*	mahs-soo'ngoo nee ee'koo

By Steamboat. (*Jōkisen de.*)

(For Vocabulary see page 37.)

English.	Japanese (romanized).	Pronunciation.
When do we start?	*Nanji goro ni shup-pan shimasŭ ka?*	nahnjee gohroh nee shoop-pahn sheemah's' kah?
Send the steward to me	*Makanai-kata wo kochira ni yoko-shĭte o-kure*	mahkahn*i*'-kah'tah woh koh-chee'rah nee yoh-koh'sh'teh oh-koo'reh
What is the first-cabin fare?	*Jōtō no chinsen wa ikura desŭ?*	j*oh*t*oh* noh cheen'sen wah eekoo'rah deh's'?
Please show me my berth	*Watakŭshi no ne-doko wo misete o-kure*	wahtah'k'shee noh neh-doh'koh woh meeseh'-teh oh-koo'reh
Is this berth taken?	*Kono ne-doko wa mō kashite oru ka?*	koh'noh neh-doh'koh wah m*oh* kah'sheeteh oh'roo kah?
[tain?	[*orimasŭ ka?*	[ohreemah's' kah?
Where is the cap-	*Senchō wa doko ni*	sench*oh*' wah doh'koh nee
I will engage the whole cabin	*Watakŭshi wa kono heya wo kari-kiri shimashō*	wahtah'k'shee wah koh'-noh heh'yah woh kah'ree-kee'ree sheemah-sh*oh*'
Put my bag in the cabin	*Te-kaban wo wata-kŭshi no heya ni irete o-kure*	teh-kah'bahn woh wah-tahk'shee noh heh'yah nee eereh'teh oh-koo'reh
Have you a pass-port?	*Ryokō-menjō wo o mochi de gozai-masŭ ka?*	ree-ohk*oh*' - menj*oh*' woh oh moh'chee deh goh-z*i*-mah's' kah?
What is the number of your cabin?	*Nan-gō no shitsu ni irasshaimasŭ?*	nahn-ng*oh* noh shee'tsoo nee eerahs-sh*i*-mah's'?
I am in number three	*San-gō ni orimasŭ*	sahn-ng*oh* nee ohree-mah's'

English.	Japanese (romanized).	Pronunciation.
Will it be rough?	*Kōkai ni wa umi ga aremashō ka?*	koh'ki nee wah oo'mee gah ahreh-mashoh' kah?
The sea is rough	*Umi ga arai n' desŭ*	oo'mee gah ah'ri n' deh's'
Is she a good boat?	*Kono fune wa yoi fune desŭ ka?*	koh'noh foo'neh wah yoy foo'neh deh's' kah?
Shall you stay on deck?	*Kampan ni nokotte oide deshō ka?*	kahm'pahn nee nohkoht'-teh oy'deh dehshoh' kah?
No, I shall go below	*Iiye, watakŭshi wa shĭta ye ikimasŭ*	ee'yeh, wahtah'k'shee wah sh'tah yeh eekeemah's'
I feel very sick	*Watakŭshi wa taisō mukatsukimasŭ*	wahtah'k'shee wah ti-soh' mookahtsookeemah's'
I am going below to my cabin	*Watakŭshi wa heya ye mairimasŭ*	wahtah'k'shee wah heh'-yah yeh mi-reemah's'
Can we have dinner on board?	*Fune ni yashoku ga arimasŭ ka?*	foo'neh nee yah-shoh'koo gah ahreemah's' kah?
Open (shut) the port-hole	*Mado wo akete (shimete) o-kure*	mah'doh woh ahkeh'teh (sheemeh'teh)oh-koo'reh
Here! Boatman!	*Oi! Sendo!*	oy! sen'doh!
How much to take me ashore?	*Oka made ikura de nosete kureru ka?*	oh'kah mah'deh eekoo'-rah deh nohseh'teh koo-reh'roo kah?
Please let me see your passport	*Go-menjō wo chotto o mise nasŭtte kudasai*	goh-menjoh' woh choht'-toh oh mee'seh nah'-s(oo)t-teh koodahsi'

Arrival. (*Tō-chaku.*)

(See Vocabulary 21, page 35.)

English.	Japanese (romanized).	Pronunciation.
Here is my luggage	*Watakŭshi no nimotsŭ wa koko ni aru*	wahtah'k'shee noh nee-moh'ts' wah koh'koh nee ah'roo
Where is the custom-house?	*Zeikwan wa doko desŭ ka?*	zay'kwahn wah doh'koh deh's' kah?
Bring that trunk to the custom-house	*Chotto Zeikwan made sono kaban wo motte koi*	choht'toh zay'kwan mah'-deh soh'noh kah'bahn woh moht'teh koy
Have you anything to declare? [dutiable	*Kaban no naka ni nani ka zei wo osamu-beki mono ga gozaimasŭ ka?*	kah'bahn noh nah'kah nee nah'nee kah zay woh oh-sah'moo-beh'kee moh'-noh gah goh-zi-mah's' kah?
I have nothing	*Iiye, gozaimasen*	ee'yeh, goh-zi-mah'sen

English.	Japanese (romanized).	Pronunciation.
Please give me your keys	*Kagi wo kashĭte kudasai*	kah'nghee woh kah'-sh(ee)teh koodahsi'
Here are the keys	*Kagi wa koko ni gozaimasŭ*	kah'nghee wah koh'koh nee goh-zi-mah's'
Is there an omnibus?	*Nori-ai-basha ga arimasŭ ka?*	noh'ree-i-bah'shah gah ahreemah's' kah?
Call a carriage	*Basha wo tanonde o-kure*	bah'shah woh tahnohn'-deh oh-koo'reh
There is no carriage	*Basha wa gozaimasen*	bah'shah wah gohzimah'sen
What is the fare to the hotel?	*Yado-ya made no chinsen wa ikura desŭ?*	yah'doh-yah mah'deh noh cheen'sen wah eekoo'-rah deh's'?
Tell the driver where to take me	*Yuku tokoro wo gyosha ni mōshĭte o-kure*	yoo'koo tohkoh'roh woh ghee-oh'shah nee moh'-sh'teh oh-koo'reh

The Hotel. (Jap., *Yadoya;* foreign, *Hōteru.*)

(See Vocabulary 13, page 21.)

English.	Japanese (romanized).	Pronunciation.
Is the proprietor anywhere about?	*Teishi wa kochira de gozaimasŭ ka?*	tay'shee wah koh-chee'-rah deh gohzimah's' kah
Have you a room vacant?	*Zashĭki wa aite imasŭ ka?*	zah'sh'kee wah i'teh ee-mah's' kah?
I want two or three rooms	*Watakŭshi wa heya wo futa mi ma irimasŭ*	wahtah'k'shee wah heh'-yah woh foo'tah mee mah eereemah's'
Have you a larger room?	*Motto okii heya ga gozaimasŭ ka?*	moht'toh ohkee' heh'yah gah goh-zi-mah's kah?
This room is too small	*Kono heya wa ammari chiisai*	koh'noh heh'yah wah ahm-mah'ree chee-si'
Show me a bedroom	*Nema wo misete o-kure*	neh'mah woh meeseh'teh oh-koo'reh
I will take this one	*Kore wa karimashō*	koh'reh wah kahreemah-shoh'
Have you no better ones?	*Motto ii no wa arimasen ka?*	moht'toh ee noh wah ah-reemah'sen kah?
Have you not a cooler room?	*Motto suzushii tokoro wa arimasen ka?*	moht'toh soo-dzooshee' tohkoh'roh wah ahree-mah'sen kah?
I want a large one	*Okii no ga hoshii*	ohkee' noh gah hoh-shee'
Show me some nice rooms	*Ii heya wo misete o-kure*	ee heh'yah woh meeseh'-teh oh-koo'reh

English.	Japanese (romanized).	Pronunciation.
How much do you charge per day?	*Ichi-nichi no tomari-ryō wa ikura?*	ee'chee-nee'chee noh toh-mah'ree-ree-*oh'* wah ee-koo'rah?
Has my luggage [come?	*Nimotsŭ wa maitta* [*ka?*	neemoh'ts' wah mi't-tah [kah?
Send the luggage upstairs	*Nimotsŭ wo nikai ye agesasete kure*	neemoh'ts' woh neeki' yeh ah-ngeh-sahseh'teh koo'reh
Put it down here	*Koko ye oite kudasai*	koh'koh yeh oy'teh koo-[dahsi'
Do you intend to stay long?	*Nagaku go toryū nasaimasŭ ka?*	nah-ngah'koo goh tohree-oo' nahsi-mah's' kah?
I shall stay a few days	*Ryō-san-nichi tomaru*	ree-*oh'*-sahn-nee'chee tohmah'roo
I want to have a [wash	*Chōdzu wo tsukaitai*	choh'dzoo woh tsooki-ti'
I want something to eat	*Nani ka tabetai*	nah'nee kah tahbeh-ti'
Anything will do	*Nan demo yoroshii*	nahn deh'moh yohroh-[sh*ee*
A decanter of water	*Midzu tokkuri*	mee'dzoo tohk-koo'ree
Give me the key of my room	*Heya no kagi wo o-kure*	heh'yah noh kah-nghee woh oh-koo'reh
What are the hours for meals here?	*Kochira de wa, gozen no jikoku wa, nan-ji to nan-ji desŭ?*	koh-chee'rah deh wah, goh-zen noh jeekoh'koo wah, nahnjee toh nahn-jee deh's'?
Luncheon is at..., and dinner at...	*He! o hiru wa...de, o yashoku ga ...de gozaimasŭ*	heh! oh hee'roo wah... deh, oh yahshoh'koo gah ...deh goh-zi-mah's'
There is no fixed time	*He! asa wa, kimari ga gozaimasen*	heh! ah'sah wah, kee-mah'ree gah goh-zi-mah'sen
And breakfast?	*Sore de wa, asa-han* [*wa?*	soh'reh deh wah, ah'sah-[hahn wah?
You can suit your own convenience	*Anata no go tsugō shidai*	ahnah'tah noh goh tsoo-ngoh' sheedi'
Can I dine in my room?	*Jibun no heya de shokuji suru koto ga dekimasŭ ka?*	jee'boon noh heh'yah deh shoh-koo'jee soo-roo koh-toh gah deh-kee-mah's' kah?
Are the beds well-aired?	*Kono yagu wa yoku kawa-kashĭte aru ka?* [*desŭ?*	koh'noh yah'ngoo wah yoh'koo kahwah-kah'sh'-teh ah-roo kah? [deh's'?
Where is the w.c.?	*Benjo wa dochira*	benjoh wah dohcheerah

English	Japanese (romanized).	Pronunciation.
I suppose you have baths here?	*Uchi ni furo-ba ga aru darō?*	oo'chee nee foo'roh-bah gah ah'roo dahroh?
I want a warm bath	*Yu ni hairitai*	yoo nee hi-reeti' [reh
Give me some soap	*Shabon wo o-kure*	shah'bohn woh oh-koo'-
Give me a towel	*Taoru wo o-kure*	tahoh'roo woh oh-koo'reh
Where is the bell?	*Rin wa doko desŭ?*	reen wah doh'koh deh's'?
Can you lend me some slippers?	*Surippa wo is-soku kashĭte kureru ka?*	sooreep'pah woh ees-soh'-koo kah'sh'teh kooreh'-roo kah? [dah
I want a candle	*Rōsoku wo iriyō da*	roh'sohkoo woh eeree-yoh'
I think of leaving to-morrow	*Myōnichi shuttatsu shimashō*	mee-oh' neechee shoot-tah'tsoo sheemah-shoh'
Call me early in the morning	*Asa hayaku okoshĭte moraitai*	ah'sah hah-yah'koo oh-koh'sh'teh mohri-ti'
It is chilly to-night	*Konya wa yohodo samui n' da*	kohn'yah wah yohhoh'-doh sah-moo'ee n' dah
Put on more bed-clothes	*Yagu wo motto kakete o-kure*	yah'ngoo woh moht'toh kah-keh'teh oh-koo'reh
Send "Boots" to me	*Rōka-ban wo kochira ni yokoshĭte o-kure*	roh'kah-bahn woh koh-chee'rah nee yohkoh-sh'teh oh-koo'reh
What do you require, sir? [water	*O atsuraye wa nanĭ de gozaimasŭ?*	oh ahtsoorah'yeh wah nah'n' deh gohzimah's'?
Give me some hot	*Yu wo o-kure*	yoo woh oh-koo'reh
Clean my shoes	*Kutsŭ wo migaite moraitai* [tai	koo'ts' woh mee-nghi'teh mohri-ti' [mohri-ti'
I want a shave	*Hige wo sutte morai-*	hee'ngeh woh soot'teh
Is there a barber about here?	*Koko ni tokoya ga arimasŭ ka?*	koh'koh nee tohkoh'yah gah ahreemah's' kah?
Send my boots to be repaired	*Kutsŭ wo naoshi ni yatte o-kure*	koot's' woh nah-oh'shee nee yaht'teh oh-koo'reh
Let this linen go to the laundry	*Kono mono wo sen-taku-ya ye dashĭte moraitai*	koh'noh moh'noh woh sentah'koo-yah yeh dahsh'teh mohri-ti'
My clothes are wet	*Kimono-ga nurete imasŭ*	keemohnoh-ngah noo-reh'teh eemah's'
Please dry them	*Yoku kawakashĭte o-kure*	yoh'koo kahwahkah'sh'-teh oh-koo'reh
Brush my clothes	*Kimono wo burashi wo kakete o-kure*	keemoh'noh woh boorah'-shee woh kahkehteh oh- [koo'reh

English.	Japanese (romanised).	Pronunciation.
Are you going to change your clothes, sir?	*O meshi-mono wo o ki-kae nasaimasŭ ka?*	oh meh'shee-moh'noh woh oh kee-kah'eh nah-*si*-mah's' kah?
Let us have the bill	*Dōka, kanjō-gaki wo motte kite o-kure*	d*oh*'kah, kahnj*oh*'-ngah'-kee woh moht'teh kee'-teh oh-koo'reh
Is the luggage ready?	*Nimotsŭ no shitaku wa ii ka?*	neemoh'ts' noh sheetah'-koo wah *ee* kah?
Send the luggage to the station	*Nimotsŭ wo suteishon ye yatte o-kure*	neemoh'ts' woh sootay'-shohn yeh yaht'teh oh-koo'reh
Take me to the station	*Suteishon made nosete yatte kure*	sootay'shohn mah'deh nohsehteh yahtteh kooreh

Meals. (*Shokuji no koto.*)

(See Vocabularies 13 & 14, pages 24 & 25.)

English.	Japanese (romanised).	Pronunciation.
Show me the bill of fare	*Kondate wo misete o-kure*	kohndah'teh woh mee-seh'teh oh-koo'reh
Please bring tea and cakes	*O cha to kwashi wo motte koi*	oh chah toh kwah'shee woh moht'teh koy
What is your order?	*O atsuraye wa nan de gozaimasŭ?*	oh ahtsoorah'yeh wah nahn deh gohz*i*-mah's'?
Please make me some tea	*Cha wo irete o-kure*	chah woh eereh'teh oh-koo'reh
I will make the tea myself	*Watakŭshi wa jibun de cha wo koshiraeru*	wahtah'k'shee wah jee'-boon deh chah woh koh-sheerah-eh'roo
I am hungry	*O naka ga sŭkimashĭta*	oh nah'kah gah s'kee-mah'sh'tah
I am thirsty	*Nodo ga kawakimashĭta*	noh'doh gah kahwahkee-mah'sh'tah
It is quite uneatable	*Mazukŭte taberarenai*	mahdzoo'k'teh tabehrah-rehn*i*'
—— undrinkable	*Mazukŭte nomenai*	mahdzoo'k'teh nohmeh-[n*i*'
This is quite enough	*Kore de takŭsan*	koh'reh deh tah'k'sahn
May I offer you some fish?	*Sakana wa ikaga de gozaimasŭ?*	sahkah'nah wah eekah'-ngah deh goh-z*i*-mah's'?
Thanks, I will take some	*Hai, chodai itashimashō*	h*i*, chohd*i*' eetahshee-mahsh*oh*'
I am not fond of [potatoes	*Imo ga kirai desŭ*	ee'moh gah kee-r*i* deh's'?

English.	Japanese (romanized).	Pronunciation.
It looks tasty	*Oishisō desŭ*	oy-sheesoh' deh's'
Which do you prefer?	*Dore ga yoroshiu gozaimasŭ?*	doh'reh gah yohrohshee'-oo goh-zi-mah's'?
I prefer roast to boiled	*Nita no yori wa yaketa no yoroshiu gozaimasŭ*	nee'tah noh yoh'ree wah yahkeh'tah no yohroh shee'oo goh-zi-mah's'
Either will do	*Sore wa dochira de mo yoroshii*	soh'reh wah doh-chee'rah deh moh yoh'rohshee'
I have nothing to eat	*Taberu mono ga nai*	tahbeh'roo moh'noh gah ni
Is the soup ready?	*Sōppu ga dekita ka?*	sohp'poo gah dehkee'tah [kah?
Dinner is ready (served)	*Gozen ga dekimashĭta*	goh'zen gah deh-keemah'-sh'tah [kah?
Do you like...?	*...ga o suki desŭ ka?*	...gah oh soo'kee deh's'
I must have them fresh [please	*Atarashiku nai no wa iranai*	ahtahrahshee'koo ni noh wah eerahni'
Give me a little,	*Sukoshi o-kure*	sookoh'shee oh-koo'reh
There is none left	*Mō mina ni narimashĭta*	moh mee'nah nee nah-reemah'sh'tah
Will you pass the mustard?	*Karashi wo o-kure?*	kahrah'shee woh oh-koo'-reh
Another cup of tea	*Cha wa mō ippai*	chah wah moh eep-pi'
Give me some more sugar (milk)	*Satō (chichi) wo motto o-kure*	sahtoh' (chee'chee) woh moht'toh oh-koo'reh
Put some more water in the teapot	*Dobin ye yu wo motto sashĭte o-kure*	doh'been yeh yoo woh moht'toh sah'sh'teh oh-koo'reh
Bring me the tea-pot	*Dobin wo motte kite o-kure*	doh'been woh moht'teh kee'teh oh-koo'reh
Have you any fresh butter?	*Deki-tate no bata ga arimasŭ ka?*	deh'kee-tah'teh noh bah'-tah gah ahreemah's' kah?
What fish have you?	*Dō iŭ sakana ga aru?*	doh ee-oo' sahkah'nah gah ah'roo?
I will take some fish	*Sakana wo tabemashō*	sahkah'nah woh tahbeh-mahshoh'
Waiter, some bread	*Kyuji, pan wo o-kure*	kee-oo'jee, pahn woh oh-koo'reh
What wine will you take, sir?	*Sake wa, nani ga yoroshiŭ gozaimasŭ?*	sah'keh wah nah'nee gah yohrohshee-oo' goh-zi-mah's'?

English.	Japanese (romanized).	Pronunciation
Open the bottle and bring it here	*Tokkuri wo akete motte koi*	tohk-koo'ree woh ahkeh'-teh moht'teh koy
Show me the wine list	*Sake no hyō wo misete o-kure*	sah'keh noh hee-*oh'* woh meeseh'teh oh-koo'reh
Have you English beer?	*Igirisu-biiru wa arimasŭ ka?*	ee-ngheeree'soo-bee'roo wah ahreemah's' kah?
What meat is there?	*Niku-rui wa nani-ga aru ka?*	nee'koo-roo'ee wah nah'-nee-ngah ah'roo kah?
Give me a slice of ham	*Hamu wo shĭto-kiri o-kure*	hah'moo woh sh'toh-kee'-ree oh-koo'reh
Have you any roast beef?	*Yaki-ushi ga aru ka?*	yah'kee-oo'shee gah ah'-roo kah?
Do you prefer well-done or under-done?	*Yoku yaita no-ga o suki desŭ ka, namayaki wo o konomi desŭ ka?*	yoh'koo *yi*'tah noh-ngah oh soo'kee deh's' kah, nahmah-yah'kee woh oh kohnoh'mee deh's' kah?
What will you take now?	*Kore kara nani wo sashi-agemashō ka?*	koh'reh kah'rah nah'nee woh sah'shee-ah-ngheh-mahsh*oh'* kah? [shee
A little of the fat	*Shiromi wo sukoshi*	sheeroh'mee woh sookoh'-
Give me some lean	*Akami no tokoro wo o-kure*	ah-kah'mee noh tohkoh'-roh woh oh-koo'reh
Pass me the sauce	*Sōsu wo o-kure*	*soh*-soo woh oh-koo'reh
Will you carve that fowl?	*Sono tori wo kitte kurenai ka?*	soh'noh toh'ree woh keet'teh koorehn*i*' kah?
Change my plate	*Sara wo tori-kaete o-kure*	sah'rah woh toh'ree-kah-eh'teh oh-koo'reh
Will you have some potatoes?	*Imo wa ikaga de gozaimasŭ ka?*	ee'moh wah eekah'ngah deh goh-*zi*-mah's' kah?
Boiled potatoes; roasted potatoes	*Udeta-imo; yaki-imo*	oodeh'tah-ee'moh; yah'-kee-ee'moh [nahs*i*'
Hand me your plate	*Sara wo okashi nasai*	sah'rah woh oh-kah'shee
I will not take any	*Itadakimasen*	eetahdahkeemah'sen
I should like some buttered toast	*Bata-yaki pan wo o-kure*	bah'tah-yah'kee pahn woh oh-koo'reh
Shall I bring you some more?	*Mō sukoshi sashia-gemashō ka?*	m*oh* sookoh'shee sahshee-ah-ngheh-mahsh*oh'* kah?
No, thank you, I can't eat any more	*Arigatō, mō takŭ-san itadakima-shĭta*	ahree-ngaht*oh'*, m*oh* tahk'sahn eetahdahkee-mah'sh'tah

The Time. (*Jikoku.*)

(See Vocabulary 8, page 18.)

NOTE.—(1) The Japanese do not generally say "twenty minutes to four," or "a quarter to six," &c., but almost invariably state the minutes past the hour. For example, "twenty minutes to four" is expressed as "forty minutes past three," and "a quarter to six" as "forty-five minutes past five."

(2) A.M. is expressed by prefixing the word "*gosen*," and P.M. by the word "*go-go*."

English.	Japanese (romanized).	Pronunciation.
What time is it?	*Mō nan-ji desŭ?*	mo*h* nahn-jee deh's'?
It is eight o'clock	*Hachi-ji de gozai-masŭ*	hah'chee-jee deh goh-zi-mah's'
Half-past nine	*Ku-ji han*	koo-jee hahn
A quarter to twelve	*Jū-ni-ji jū-go-fun mae*	j*oo*-nee-jee j*oo*-goh-foon mah'eh
Twenty minutes past one	*Ichi-ji ni-jip-pun*	ee'chee-jee nee-jeep-poon
Ten minutes to two	*Ichi-ji go jip-pun*	ee'chee-jee goh jeep-poon
A quarter past four	*Yo-ji jū-go-fun*	yoh-jee j*oo*-goh-foon
It is just about noon	*Kare kore hiru desŭ*	kah'reh koh'reh hee'roo deh's'
10 a.m.	*Go-zen-jū-ji*	goh-zen-j*oo*-jee
11 p.m.	*Go-go-jū-ichi-ji*	goh-ngoh-j*oo*-ee'chee-jee
It commences at half-past one	*Ichi-ji han ni haji-marimasŭ*	ee'chee-jee hahn nee hahjeemahreemah's'
I will come to-morrow	*Miōnichi mairimasŭ*	meeo*h*'neechee m*i*-ree-mah's'
Early in the morning	*Asa hayaku*	ah'sah hah-yah'koo
It must be late	*Mō osok'arō*	moh oh-sohk'ahro*h*'
Every other day	*Ichi nichi oki*	ee'chee nee'chee oh'kee
Day after to-morrow	*Myōgonichi*	mee-*oh*'ngoh-neechee
Day before yesterday	*Issakujitsu*	ees-sah-koojee'tsoo
Half-an-hour	*Han-ji-kan*	hahn-jee-kahn
An hour and a half	*Ichi-ji-han kan*	ee'chee-jee-hahn kahn
For a short time	*Sukoshi no aida*	sookoh'shee noh *i*'dah
At any time	*Nandoki demo*	nahndoh'kee deh'moh
At the same time	*Dō-ji ni*	do*h*-jee nee

The Weather. (*Tenki.*)

(See Vocabularies 1 & 2, pages 13 & 14.)

It is fine weather	*Yoi o tenki de gozai-masŭ*	yoy oh ten'kee deh goh-z*i*-mah's'
It is most disagreeable weather	*Komarimashĭta o tenki desŭ*	kohmahreemah'sh'tah oh ten'kee deh's'

English.	Japanese (romanized).	Pronunciation.
It is really beautiful weather	*Makoto ni kekkō na o tenki desŭ*	mahkoh'toh nee kek-*koh'* nah oh ten'kee deh's'
I am knocked up by this heat	*Kono atsŭsa ni dōmo yowarimashĭta*	koh'noh ah'ts'sah nee d*oh'*moh yoh-wah-ree-mah'sh'tah
The heat is unbearable to-day	*Kyō no atsŭsa wa, koraeraremasen* [*nai*	kee-*oh'* noh ah'ts'sah wah, kohrah-eh-rahreh-mah'-sen [ni
It is terribly hot	*Atsŭkute shi-yō ga*	ahts'koo'teh shee-*yoh*gah
I will come to-morrow if fine	*Miōnichi tenki ga yoroshĭ-kereba, mairimasŭ*	mee-*oh'*neechee ten'kee gah yohroh'sh'-kehreh'-bah m*i*-reemah's'
Can you lend me an umbrella?	*Kōmori-gasa wo kashĭte kudasai-masŭ ka?*	k*oh'*mohree-ngah'sah woh kah'sh'teh koo-dah-s*i*-mah's' kah
Is it raining?	*Ame wa futte imasŭ ka?* [*imasŭ*	ah'meh wah foot'teh ee-mah's' kah? [eemah's'
It is raining a little	*Furu ni wa futte*	foo'roo nee wah foot'teh
It looks as if the rain would clear off	*Ame ga agarisō desŭ*	ah'meh gah ah-ngahree-*soh* deh's'
We were (*or*, I was) kept in by the rain	*Ame ni furi-komare-mashĭta*	ah'meh nee foo'ree-koh-mah'reh-mah'-sh'tah
It seems likely to	*Ame ga furisō da*	ah'meh gah fooreeso*h* dah
It is snowing [rain	*Yuki ga furimasŭ*	yoo'kee gah fooreemah's'

Health. (*Karada no ambai.*)

(For Vocabulary see page 23.)

I feel ill	*Kagen ga warŭ go-zaimasŭ*	kah'nghen gah wahr*oo'* goh-zi-mah's' [mah's'
I have a sore throat	*Nodo ga itamimasŭ*	noh'doh gah eetahmee-
I have a headache	*Zutsŭ ga shimasŭ*	dzootso*o'* gah sheemah's'
I have caught cold	*Kaze wo hĭkimashĭta*	kah'zeh woh h(ee)kee-mah'sh'tah
I have a pain in my back	*Senaka ga itami-masŭ*	sehnah'kah gah eetah-meemah's'
I have a bad cough	*Hidoku seki ga demasŭ*	heedoh'koo seh'kee gah deh-mah's' [mah's'
I have a pain here	*Koko ga itamimasŭ*	koh'koh gah eetahmee-
You had better consult the doctor	*Isha ni mite morau ga yokarō*	ee'shah nee mee'teh moh-row' gah yohkahr*oh'*

English.	Japanese (romanized).	Pronunciation.
Please call a good doctor for me	*Dōzo yoi isha wo sagashĭte kudasai*	doh'zoh yoy ee'shah woh sah-ngah'sh'teh koodahsi
He will come immediately [come	*Mō jiki kimasŭ*	moh jee'kee keemah's' [mah'sh'tah
The doctor has	*Isha-ga miemashĭta*	ee'shah-ngah mee-eh-
I wish to consult you [pulse	*Go shinsatsŭ wo negaimasŭ*	goh sheensah'ts' woh neh-nghi-mah's' [ken
Let me feel your	*O myaku wo haiken*	oh mee-ah'koo woh hi'-
How do you feel to-day?	*Go byōki wa ikaga de gozaimasŭ?*	goh beeoh'kee wah eekah'-ngah deh gohzimah's'
Much better, thanks	*Arigatō gozaimasŭ. Ōki ni kokoro-yoku narimashĭta*	ahree-ngah-toh' goh-zi-mah's'; oh'kee nee koh-koh'roh yoh'koo nah-reemah'sh'tah
Have it made up at a chemist's	*Kono kusuri no chōgō wa kusu-riya ni sasena-kereba ikemasen*	koh'noh koosoo'ree noh choh-ngoh wah koosoo-ree'yah nee sahsehnah-kehreh'bah eekehmah'- [sen
Where is there a chemist's shop?	*Kusuri-ya wa doko desŭ ka?*	koosoo'ree-yah wah doh'koh deh's' kah?
Here is the medicine	*Kore wa kusuri de gozaimasŭ*	koh'reh wah koosoo'ree deh goh-zi-mah's'
This medicine is to be taken three times a day	*Kono kusuri wa ichi nichi sando dzutsu nomu no desŭ*	koh'noh koosoo'ree wah ee'chee nee'chee sahn'-doh dzoo'tsoo noh'moo noh dehs'

Correspondence. The Post-office. Telegrams.*

(*Shokan. Yūbin. Dempō.*)

(For Vocabularies see pages 45, 46.)

English.	Japanese (romanized).	Pronunciation.
Have no letters come this morning? [come	*Kesa, yūbin wa kimasen ka?*	keh'sah, yoo'been wah keemah'sen kah?
No, none have	*He! mairimasen*	heh! mi-reemah'sen
I have not received a letter (letters)	*Tegami wa hĭtotsŭ mo konai*	teh-ngah'mee wah sh(ee)-toht's' moh kohni'
Please post this letter	*Kono tegami wo dashĭte o-kure*	koh'noh teh-ngah'mee woh dah'sh'teh ohkoo'reh

* No difficulty will be found in transacting postal or telegraphic business in Japan, as the routine is modelled upon English methods.

English.	Japanese (romanized).	Pronunciation.
He ought to be here by now	*Mō kuru hazu da-ga!*	moh koo'roo hah'dzoo dah-ngah!
I have heard noth- [ing	*Tonto kikimasen*	tohn'toh keekeemah'sen
Has the mail steamer arrived?	*Yūbin sen wa tō-chaku shimashĭta ka?*	yoo'been sen wah *toh'*-chahkoo sheemah'sh'-tah kah?
Go and see if the mail is (letters are) in	*Yūbin ga haitta ka itte mite o-kure*	*yoo'*been gah h*i*'t-tah-kah eet'teh mee'teh oh-koo'-reh
Are there any letters for me?	*Watakŭshi ni ateta tegami ga gozai-masŭ ka?*	wahtah'k'shee nee ah-teh'tah teh-ngah'mee gah goh-*zi*-mah's' kah?
Please forward my letters to...	*Watakŭshi ni ateta tegami wa ... ye todokete kudasai*	wahtahk'shee nee ahteh-tah teh-ngahmee wah... yeh tohdohkehteh koodahs*i*'
Please weigh this letter (these letters)	*Kono tegami no mekata wo kakete mite kudasai*	koh'noh teh-ngah'mee noh mehkah'teh woh kah-keh'teh mee'teh koodahs*i*'
How much is the postage on this letter (these letters)?	*Kono tegami no yū-binzei wa ikura kakarimasŭ ka?*	kohnoh teh-ngahmee noh yoobeenzay wah eekoo-rah kahkahreemahs' kah?
This letter is to be registered	*Kono tegami wo kakitome ni shĭte o-kure*	koh'noh teh-ngah'mee woh kahkee-toh'meh nee sh'teh oh-koo'reh
Receipt for registered letter	*Kaki-tome no uke-tori*	kah'kee-toh'meh noh oo'-keh-toh'ree
A registered letter	*Kaki-tome no tega-[mi*	kah'kee-toh'meh noh teh-[ngah'mee
I am just going to read it	*Nan'da ka kore kara yomu tokoro desŭ*	nahn' dah kah koh'reh kah'rah yoh'moo toh-koh'roh deh's'
Tell him to wait	*Matashĭte kudasai*	mahtah'sh'teh koodahs*i*'
I will send a reply later	*Ato kara go aisatsu wo mōshimashō*	ah'toh kah'rah goh *i*-sah'-tsoo woh *moh*sheemah-sh*oh*
Can I send a tele- [gram?	*Dempō wo yarare- [masŭ ka?*	demp*oh'* woh yahrahreh- [mah's' kah?
I have received a telegram from...	*...kara dempō ga kimashĭta*	...kah'rah demp*oh'* gah keemah'sh'tah
Has a telegram come for me?	*Watakŭshi ni ateta dempō-ga kima-shĭta ka?*	wahtah'k'shee nee ah-teh'tah demp*oh'*-ngah keemah'sh'tah kah?

English.	Japanese (romanized).	Pronunciation.
Please send this telegram	*Kono dempō wo dashite kudasai*	koh'noh demp*oh'* woh dah'sh'teh koodahs*i'*
I want a postal order	*Yūbin-kawase wo negaitō gozaimasŭ*	*yoo'*been-kahwahseh woh neh-ngh*i*-t*oh'* gohz*i*mahs'
The payee's name and address is...	*Kawase-kin uketori-nin no shukusho to seimei wa...*	kahwah'seh-keen ookeh-tohreeneen noh shookoo-shoh toh saymay' wah...
The sender's name and address is...	*Sashi-dashi-nin no seimei, shukusho wa...*	sah'shee-dah'shee-neen noh saymay', shookoo'-shoh wah...
I am the sender	*Watakŭshi wa sashi-dashi-nin de gozaimasŭ*	wahtah'k'shee wah sah'-shee-dah'shee-neen deh goh-z*i*-mah's'
Please cash this money-order (postal-order)	*Kono kawase-kin wo negaitō gozai-masŭ*	koh'noh kah-wah'seh-keen woh neh-ngh*i*-t*oh'* goh-z*i*-mah's'

Introductions. (*Shō-kai.*)

English.	Japanese (romanized).	Pronunciation.
Allow me to introduce Mr. ...	*Kono o kata wa ... San to osshai-masŭ. O hiki-awase itashimasŭ*	koh'noh oh kah'tah wah ...sahn toh ohssh*i*mah's'; oh hee'kee-ahwah'seh eetahsheemah's'
Kindly give me a letter of introduction to Mr....	*Osore-irimasŭ ga... San ye go tensho wo kudasaimasen ka?*	ohsohreh-eereemahs' gah ...sahn yeh goh tenshoh woh koodahs*i*mahsen kah
Here is the letter of introduction to him	*Kore wa tensho de gozaimasŭ*	koh'reh wah ten'shoh deh goh-z*i*-mah's'
Allow me to introduce myself to you; my name is...	*Watakŭshi wa ... to mōsu mono de go-zaimasŭ*	wahtah'k'shee wah...toh m*oh'*soo moh'noh deh goh-z*i*-mah's'
Please introduce me to Mr....	*...San ye o hiki-awase kudasaima-sen ka?*	...sahn yeh oh hee'kee-ahwah'seh koodahs*i*-mah'sen kah?
I beg to introduce Mr. ..., a friend of mine	*Konata wa ... San to iū, watakŭshi no hōyū de go-zaimasŭ*	kohnah'tah wah ... sahn toh ee-*oo'*, wahtah'k'shee noh h*oh*-*yoo* deh goh-z*i*-mah's'
Here is my card	*Kore wa watakŭshi no meishi de gozai-masŭ*	koh'reh wah wahtah'k'-shee noh may'shee deh goh-z*i*-mah's'

English.	Japanese (romanized).	Pronunciation.
Pleased to make your acquaintance	*Hajimemashĭte o me ni kakari-masŭ*	hahjeemehmah'sh'teh oh meh nee kahkahreemahs'
I trust you will honour me with your continued friendship	*Iku-hisashiku go kon-i wo negai-masŭ*	ee'koo-heesah-shee'koo goh kohn-ee woh neh-nghi-mah's'
I will call again	*Mata agarimashō*	mah'tah ah-ngahreemah-shoh'

In Town; Visiting. (*Shichū de; Mimai.*)

(For Vocabulary, see page 28.)

NOTE.—For hiring conveyances see "Travelling by Road," p. 83; see also "Enquiries," p. 79; and "Shopping," p. 101.

English.	Japanese (romanized).	Pronunciation.
What shall we do?	*Dō shimashō?*	doh sheemahshoh'?
Very well; come along	*Sa! oide nasaimashi*	sah! oy'deh nah-si-mah'-shee
Am I wrong to have come at this time?	*Ima jibun maitta no ga warui no desŭ ka?*	ee'mah jee'boon mi't-tah noh gah wahroo'ee noh deh's' kah?
Excuse my having kept you waiting	*O machidō sama*	oh mahcheedoh' sah'mah
You wait here	*Omaye koko ni matte ore*	ohmah'yeh koh'koh nee maht'teh oh'reh
Suppose we go?	*Itcha dō desu?*	eet'chah doh deh's'?
I am tired; let us rest a little	*Kŭtabiremashĭta kara chotto yasumimashō*	k'tah-beereh-mah'sh'tah kah'rah choht'toh yah-soomeemahshoh'
I am tired out	*Kŭtabirete shi-yō ga nai*	k'tahbeereh'teh shee-yoh gah ni
Take care! (look out!)	*Ki wo tsukero!* (blunt)	kee woh tsookeh'roh!
Take care of yourself!	*O daiji ni asobase!*	oh di'jee nee ahsohbah'-seh!
I say! (Hallo there!)	*Are sa!*	ah'reh sah!
Where are you going?	*Omaye wa doko ye iku no da?* (fam.)	ohmah'yeh wah doh'koh yeh ee'koo noh dah?
I am going out now for a walk	*Kore kara undō ni dekakemasŭ*	koh'reh kah'rah oondoh' nee deh-kahkehmah's'
I should like to accompany you	*O tomo itashimashō*	oh toh'moh eetahshee-mahshoh'
I was waiting for you	*O machi mōshite orimashĭta*	oh mah'chee moh'sheeteh ohreemah'sh'tah
I was just going out	*Chōdo deru tokoro deshĭta*	choh'doh deh'roo tohkoh-roh deh'sh'tah

English.	Japanese (romanized).	Pronunciation.
I shall walk as far as the post-office	*Yūbin-kyoku made aruite ikimasŭ*	yoo'been-kee-oh'koo mah'deh ahrooee'teh eekeemah's'
I will wait until this evening	*Komban made machimashō*	kohm'bahn mah'deh mahcheemah-sh*oh'*
Wait till I come	*Watakŭshi no kuru made, matte ite kudasai*	wahtah'k'shee noh koo'-roo mah'deh, maht'teh ee'teh koodahs*i'*
I cannot come	*Mairaremasenŭ*	m*i*-rahrehmahseh'n'
I am in a hurry	*Isogimasŭ*	eesoh-ngheemah's'
Be quick!	*Hayaku!*	hah-yah'koo!
What a grand sight!	*Yoi mi-harashi desŭ, ne!*	yoy mee-hahrah'shee deh's' neh!
We needn't hurry	*Isogu ni wa oyobanai*	eesoh'ngoo nee wah oh-yohbahn*i'*
Now I am at leisure	*Ima wa te-sŭki de gozaimasŭ*	ee'mah wah teh-s'kee deh goh-z*i*-mah's'
Kindly wait a little	*Sŭkoshi o machi nasai*	s'koh'shee oh mah'chee nahs*i'*
I will not wait	*Machi wa shimasenŭ*	mah'chee wah sheemah-seh'n'
I have come to borrow a hammer	*Kanadzuchi wo hai shaku ni marimashĭta*	kahnah-dzoo'chee woh h*i* shah'koo nee mahree-mah'sh'tah
I will send it back to-morrow	*Miōnichi o kayeshi mōshimasŭ*	meeo*h'*neechee oh kah-yeh'shee m*oh'*sheemah's'
We were just speaking about you	*Anata no o-uwasa wo shĭte iru tokoro deshĭta*	ahnahtah noh oh-oowah'sah woh sh'teh ee'roo tohkoh'roh deh-sh'tah
Go and tell him to be sure and come	*Kitto kuru yō ni sō itte koi*	keet'toh koo'roo y*oh* nee s*oh* eet'teh koy
I have lost my way	*Michi wo machigaeta*	mee'chee woh mah-chee-ngah-eh'tah
Direct me to...	*Michi wo oshiete kudasai...*	mee'chee woh ohshee-eh'-teh koodahs*i'*
Take the first turning to the right	*Tsugi no migi no yoko-chō ye o magan' nasai*	tsoonghee noh meenghee noh yoh'koh-ch*oh* yeh oh mah-ngah'n'nahs*i'*
Take the second turning to the left	*Hidari no ni-ban-me no yoko-chō ye o magan' nasai*	heedah'ree noh nee-bahn-meh noh yohkohch*oh* yeh oh mah-ngah'n'nah-s*i'*

English.	Japanese (romanized).	Pronunciation
It is right in front of you	*Zutto tsuki-atari de gozaimasŭ*	dzoot'toh tsoo'kee-ahtah'-ree deh goh-*zi*-mah's'
This is the shortest way	*Kore wa ichi-ban chika-michi desŭ*	koh'reh wah ee'chee-bahn chee'kah-mee'chee deh's'
This is the longest way	*Kore wa yohodo mawari-michi desŭ*	koh'reh wah yoh-hoh'doh mah-wah'ree-mee'chee deh's'
It is straight on	*Massugu de gozai-* [*masŭ*	mahs-soo'ngoo deh goh- [*zi*-mah's'
I will show you his place	*Ano hĭto no tokoro wo oshiete age-mashō*	ah'noh sh'toh' noh toh-koh'roh woh ohshee-eh'-teh ah-ngheh-mahsh*oh'*
It is only five minutes' walk	*Aruite go fun gurai shĭka kakarima-sen*	ahrooee'teh, goh foon goori' sh'kah kahkah-reemah'sen
I don't know anyone of that name	*Sō iŭ na no hĭto wo shirimasen*	*soh* ee-*oo'* nah noh sh'toh woh sheereemah'sen
I don't know where he lives	*Doko ni orimasŭ yara watakŭshi wa shirimasen*	doh'koh nee ohreemah's' yah'rah wah'tah'k'shee wah sheereemah'sen
Is your master (mistress) within?	*Danna (Oku sama) wa o uchi ka?*	dahn'nah (oh'koo sah'-mah) wah oh oo'chee kah?
No, he (she) has gone out	*Ie, o rusu de gozaimasŭ*	heh, oh roo'soo deh goh-*zi*-mah's'?
Is Mrs. ...... at home?	*Okusama wa, o uchi de gozaimasŭ ka?*	ohkoosahmah wah oh oo'-chee deh gohzimahs' kah?
Let your master know I have come	*Watakŭshi no kita koto wo danna ye shirasete o-kure*	wahtah'k'shee noh kee'-tah koh'toh woh dahn'-nah yeh sheerah-seh'teh oh-koo'reh
You had better go [and ask	*Kiite kuru ga ii*	k*ee*'teh koo'roo gah *ee*
He is at home	*Uchi ni orimasŭ*	oo'chee nee ohreemah's'
Please come in	*Kochira ye o tōri nasai*	kohchee'rah yeh oh *toh'*-ree nahsi'
Take a seat for a [minute	*Chito o kake nasai-* [*mashi*	chee'toh oh kah'keh nah- [*si*-mah'shee
Who has come?	*Donata ga o ide ni natte orimasŭ ka?* [*mashĭta ka?*	dohnah'tah gah oh ee'deh nee naht'teh ohreemah's' kah? [mah'sh'tah kah?
Has someone come?	*Donata ka mairi-*	dohnah'tah kah m*i*-ree-
A visitor has come, sir	*O kyaku sama ga miyemashĭta*	oh kee-ah'koo sah'mah ngah mee-yeh-mah'sh'tah

English.	Japanese (romanized).	Pronunciation.
Show him (her) in	*O tōshi mose*	oh t*oh*'shee moh'seh
Really it is an age since we last met [first	*Makoto ni shibaraku o me ni kakarimasen deshĭta*	mahkoh'toh nee sheebahrah'koo oh meh nee kahkahreemah'sen deh'-[sh'tah
Excuse my going	*O saki*	oh sah'kee
I have been so busy that I could not come and see you	*Isogashĭku te tsui go busata wo itashimashĭta*	eesoh-ngah'sh'koo teh tsoo'ee goh boosah'tah woh eetahsheemah'sh'tah
I must go now	*Ikanakŭ te wa narimasenŭ*	eekahnah'k' teh wah nahreemahseh'n'
Must you really go?	*Zehi okaeri ni narimasŭ ka?*	zeh-hee ohkah-ehree nee nahreemah's' kah?
Remember me to all at home	*Mina san ni dōka yoroshĭku*	mee'nah sahn nee d*oh*'-kah yohroh'sh'koo
Go in peace! (to departing guest)	*O shidzuka ni irasshaimase!*	oh shee-dzoo'kah nee eerahs-sh*i*-mah'seh!
Good bye!	*Sayō nara!*	sah-y*oh*' nah'rah!
Please come again	*Mata irasshai*	mah'tah eerahs-sh*i*'
Did anyone call while I was out?	*Rusŭ-chū ni donata mo o ide wa nakatta ka?*	roosoo'-ch*oo* nee dohnah'-tah moh oh ee'deh wah nahkaht'tah kah?
A visitor came just as you left	*Chōdo o dekake no tokoro ye, kyaku ga miemashĭta*	ch*oh*'doh oh deh-kah'keh noh toh-koh'roh yeh, kee-ah'koo gah mee-eh-mah'sh'tah [kaht'tah
I am glad I went	*Itta no wa yokatta*	eet'tah noh wah yoh-

Shopping. (*Kaimono.*)

(See Vocabularies 4, 6, 7, 13—17, pp. 15—18, 24—30.)

NOTE.—On entering a shop a gentleman should raise his hat, saying, "*Go men nasai!*" (*lit.*, "excuse me"). This is done whether the shopkeeper is a male or a female. A lady, of course, merely says "*Go men nasai!*"

English.	Japanese (romanized).	Pronunciation.
I want some silk	*Kinu ga hoshiū gozaimasŭ*	kee'noo ngah hoh-sheeoo' goh-z*i*-mah's'
This silk is very dear	*Kono kinu wa goku takai n' desŭ*	koh'noh kee'noo wah goh'koo tahk*i* n'deh's'
This material wears well	*Kono kire-ji mochi wa yoroshiu gozaimasŭ*	koh'noh kee'reh-jee moh'-chee wah yoh-roh-sh*ee*'-oo goh-z*i*-mah's' [mah's'
I will guarantee it	*O uke-ai-mōshimasŭ*	oh oo'keh-*i*-m*oh*'shee-

English.	Japanese (romanized).	Pronunciation.
I don't guarantee it	*Uke-ai-masen*	ookeh-*i*-mah'sen
Please show me some gloves	*Tebukuro wo misete kudasai*	teh-bookoo'roh woh mee-seh'teh koodahsi'
How much is this cabinet?	*Kono tansu wa, ikura desŭ?* [*desŭ?*	koh'noh tahn'soo wah, eekoo'rah deh's'? [deh's'?
May I see it?	*Chotto mitai mon'*	choht'toh mee-*ti'* mohn'
I want to see that screen [would do	*Sono byōbu wo mitai*	soh'noh bee-*oh'*boo woh meeti' [mah's'
I should think it	*Yosasō ni omoimasŭ*	yohsahs*oh'* nee ohmoy-
What is the lowest price?	*Ketchaku no tokoro wa ikura?*	keht-chah'koo noh toh-koh'roh wah eekoo'rah?
Is this vase expensive?	*Kono hana-ike wa takai no desŭ ka?*	koh'noh hah'nah-ee'keh wah tahki'noh deh's' kah?
I will select the best from among these	*Kono uchi kara, ii no wo eridashi-mashō*	koh'noh oo'chee kah'rah, *ee* noh woh eh-reedah-shee-mahsh*oh'*
May I choose for myself?	*Yori-dotte mo ii no desŭ ka?*	yoh'ree-doht'teh moh *ee* noh deh's' kah?
May I show it to you?	*O me ni kakete mo yō gozaimasŭ ka?*	oh meh nee kahkeh'teh moh y*oh* goh-zi-mah's'
[about ten		[kah?
Please give me	*Tō bakari kudasai*	t*oh* bahkah'ree koodahsi'
This suits me, but the price is too high	*Shina wa, yoroshii ga, nedan ga osoroshii takai n' desŭ* [*masen*	shee'nah wah, yoh-roh-sh*ee'* gah, neh'dahn gah oh-soh-rohsh*ee'* tahki' n'deh's'? [mah'sen
It is not new [more	*Atarashĭ ku ari-*	ahtahrah'sh' koo ahree-
I don't want any	*Mō takŭsan*	m*oh* tah'k'sahn
I have ordered it	*Atsuraete okima-shĭta*	ahtsoorah-eh'teh ohkoo-mah'sh'tah
It's cheaper (dearer) than I thought	*Omotta yori yasui* (*takai*)	ohmoht'tah yoh'ree yahsoo'ee (tahki')
This is native made	*Kore wa wasei*	koh'reh wah wah-say'
That is imported	*Are wa hakurai de gozaimasŭ*	ah'reh wah hahkoori' deh goh-zi-mah's'
This is a still better one	*Kono hō wa, nao yoroshiu gozai-masŭ*	koh'noh h*oh* wah, nah'oh yoh-roh-shee'oo goh-zi-mah's' [sen
It won't do at all	*Totemo ikemasen*	tohteh'moh eekehmah'-
I must have it	*Nakŭcha naranŭ*	nah'k'chah nahrah'n'

English.	Japanese (romanized).	Pronunciation.
How much do you require?	*Dono gurai de yoroshiu gozaimasŭ?*	doh'noh goo-ri' deh yohrohshee'oo gohzimah's'?
I will buy these	*Kore wo kaimashō*	koh'reh woh kimahshoh'
How do you like these?	*Kono mono wa ikaga de gozaimasŭ?*	koh'noh moh'noh wah eekah'ngah deh goh-zimah's'?
I don't like any of these	*Hitotsŭ mo kono-manai*	sh'toh'ts' moh kohnoh-mahni'
How much do you ask for it?	*Nedan wa ikura?*	neh'dahn wah eekoo'rah?
I can't let you have them for less	*Motto yasuku shite agerare masen*	moht'toh yah-soo'koo sh'teh ah-nghehrah'reh mah'sen
Are they really genuine?	*Kore wa homma desŭ ka?*	koh'reh wah hohm'mah deh's' kah?
Send the things to my hotel	*Watakŭshi no mono wo yadoya ye yokoshite o-kure*	wahtah'k'shee noh moh'noh woh yahdoh'yah yeh yohkoh'sh'teh ohkoo'reh

Commercial and Trading. (*Shō-gyō.*)

(For Vocabulary see page 33.)

English.	Japanese (romanized).	Pronunciation.
May I show you my samples?	*Watakŭshi no mihon wo goran kudasai mase?*	wahtah'k'shee noh mee'hohn woh goh'rahn koo-dahsi' mah'seh?
I can sell at...	*... de sashi-agemasŭ*	...deh sah'shee-ah-ngheh-mah's'
It is impossible to sell at that figure	*Totemo sono nedan de wa uraremasen*	tohteh'moh soh'noh neh'dahn deh wah oorahreh-mah'sen
We will consider the matter	*Kangaete mimashō*	kahn-ngah-eh'teh mee-mahshoh'
I will consult my partner and let you know	*Nakama-no-mono to sōdan no ue, o shirase-mōshimasu*	nahkah'mah-noh-moh'noh toh soh'dahn noh oo'eh, oh sheerah'seh-moh'sheemahsoo
I don't think my partner would consent to trade at that price	*Sono nedan de wa nakama-no-mono ga shōchi itashi-masu-mai*	soh'noh neh'dahn deh wah nahkah'mah-noh-moh'noh gah shoh'chee eetah-sheemah'soo-mi
I'm afraid I shall lose on the sale of the goods	*Nimotsŭ wo ureba son wo shi-yashinai ka to omoimasŭ*	neemoh'ts' woh ooreh'bah sohn woh shee-yah-sheeni' kah toh ohmoh-mah's'

English.	Japanese (romanized).	Pronunciation.
I will assume the liability	*Watakŭshi wa sono sekinin wo futan shimasŭ*	wahtah'k'shee wah soh'noh sehkee'neen woh foo'tahn sheemah's'
I want samples of...	*... no mihon ga irimasŭ*	...noh mee'hohn ngah eereemah's'
I want some samples	*Mihon ga irimasŭ*	mee'hohn ngah eereemah's'
We have none in [stock	*O ainiku-sama*	oh *i*-nee'koo-sah'mah
The goods are inferior to sample	*Nimotsŭ wa mihon yori warui*	neemoh'ts' wah mee'hohn yoh-ree wahroo'ee
Show me several patterns	*Iro-iro no moyō wo misete moraitai*	ee'roh-ee'roh noh mohyoh' woh meeseh'teh mohr*i-ti'*
When can you deliver if I give you an order?	*Chūmon sureba itsŭ goro shina-mono wo watashimasŭ ka?*	choo'mohn sooreh'bah ee'ts' goh'roh shee'nah-moh'noh woh wahtah-sheemah's' kah?
I cannot give you an order	*Chūmon suru koto ga dekinai*	choo'mohn soo'roo koh'toh gah dehkeen*i'*
I wish to cancel the order	*Chūmon wo tori-keshitai mon' desŭ*	choo'mohn woh toh'ree-keh-sh't*i'* mohn' deh's'
We will consult after receiving samples	*Mihon wo moratte kara, sōdan itashimashō*	mee-hohn woh mohraht'teh kah'rah, s*oh'*dahn eetahsheemash*oh'*
You must come down a great deal	*Zūtto o make nasai*	dzoot'toh oh mah'keh nahs*i'*
I can't come down	*Makarimasen*	mahkahreemah'sen
I can't buy at that figure	*Sono nedan de wa kaware nai*	soh'noh neh'dahn deh wah kahwahreh n*i*
What is your bottom price?	*Ketchaku no tokoro wa, ikura made makarimasŭ ka?*	keht-chah'koo noh toh-koh'roh wah, eekoo'rah mah'deh mahkahree-mah's' kah?
Have the goods shipped at once	*Isoide nimotsŭ wo fune ni tsumi-dasanakereba narimasen*	eesoy'deh neemoh'ts' woh foo'neh nee tsoo'mee-dahsahnahkeh-reh'bah nahreemah'sen
Have you shipped the goods?	*Nimotsŭ wo fune ni tsumi-dashĭta ka?*	neemoh'ts' woh foo'neh nee tsoo'mee-dah'sh'tah kah?

English.	Japanese (romanized).	Pronunciation.
These goods must be carefully packed	*Dōka kono mono wo minna yoku ki-wo-tsukete ni-dzukuri shite o-kure*	doh'kah koh'noh moh'noh woh meen'nah yoh'koo kee-woh-tsookeh'teh nee-dzookoo'ree shee'teh oh-koo'reh
Put this mark on the boxes	*Hako ni kono shirushi wo tsukete okure*	hah'koh nee koh'noh sheeroo'shee woh tsoo-keh'teh oh-koo'reh
The boxes must be tin-lined	*Hako no naka ni burikki wo haranakereba ikenai [desŭ*	hah'koh noh nah'kah nee booreek'kee woh hah-rahnahkeh-reh'bah ee-kehni' [deh's'
Trade is dull	*Shōbai wa fu-keiki*	shoh'bi wah foo-kay'kee
Trade is good	*Keiki ga ii n' desŭ*	kay'kee gah *ee* n' deh's'
He has become bankrupt	*Ano hĭto wa shin-dai-kagiri ni narimashĭta*	ah'noh sh'toh wah sheen-di'-kah-nghee'ree nee nahree-mah'sh'tah
There are some errors in the account	*Kanjō ni iro-iro machigai ga aru*	kahnjoh' nee ee'roh-ee'-roh mah-chee-nghi' gah ah'roo
You have over-charged me	*Omaye wa taisō kake-ne wo tsuketa ne!*	ohmah'yeh wah ti-soh' kah'keh-neh woh tsoo-keh'tah neh !
This is a clerical error	*Kore wa kanjō chigai desŭ*	koh'reh wah kahnjoh' chee-nghi' deh's'
I have deducted the errors	*Machigatta bun wo hikimashĭta*	mah-chee-ngaht'tah boon woh heekeemah'sh'tah
It is more than was arranged	*Hajime no kime yori takai*	hahjee'meh noh kee'meh yoh'ree tahki'
I want a detailed account	*Kono kanjō wo betsu-betsu ni wakete, saimitsu ni kaite moraitai*	koh'noh kahnjoh' woh beh'tsoo-beh'tsoo nee wahkeh'teh, si-mee'tsoo nee ki'teh moh-ri-ti'
Here is a cheque for the amount of your account	*Kono ko-gitte wa kanjō zumi ni watasu*	koh'noh koh-ngheet'teh wah kahnjoh' dzoo'mee nee wahtah'soo
Send in our account	*Kanjō-gaki wo okutte kudasai*	kahnjoh-ngah'kee woh oh-koot'teh koodahsi'
Will you accept a bill?	*Kawase-tegata wa dō desho!*	kahwah'seh-teh-ngah'tah wah doh deh'shoh ?

Changing Money. (*Ryōgāe.*)

English.	Japanese (romanized).	Pronunciation.
Where is there a money-changer's?	*Ryōgae-ya wa dochira de gozaimasŭ?*	ree-*oh'*-ngah eh-yah wah doh-chee'rah deh goh-*zi*-mah's'?
Can you give me change?	*Kane wa ryōgae ga dekimasŭ ka?*	kah'neh wah ree-*oh'*ngah-eh gah deh-keemah's' kah?
Yes, sir; what change do you wish?	*Hai, dekimasŭ. Dō iū kane to tori kaemashō ka?*	hi, deh-keemah's'; d*oh* ee-*oo'* kah'neh toh toh'-ree kahehmahsh*oh'* kah?
Will you give me Japanese money?	*Nihon no kane wo o-kure?*	nee'hohn noh kah'neh woh oh-koo'reh?
Please give me 10-yen Bank of Japan notes	*Nippon Ginkō no jiu yen satsŭ wo o-kure*	neep'pohn gheenk*oh'* noh jew yen sah'ts' woh oh-koo'reh
Give me the amount in...	*Taka wo...ni shĭte o-kure*	tah'kah woh...nee sh'teh' oh-koo'reh
Change this into small money, please	*Kore wo komakai zeni to tori-kaete kudasai*	koh'reh woh kohmahk*i'* zeh'nee toh tohree-kah-eh'teh koodahs*i'*
Will you cash this cheque for me?	*Kono ko gitte wo tori-kaete kudasai-masŭ ka?*	koh-noh koh-ngheet'teh woh toh'ree-kah-eh'teh koodahs*i*-mah's' kah?
What is the rate of exchange on English money?	*Igirisu to no kawase sōba wa dō narimasŭ?*	ee-ngheeree'soo toh noh kahwah'seh s*oh'*bah wah d*oh* nahreemah's'?
Please change me an English bank-note	*Igirisu no ginkō-shihei wo tori-kaete kudasaimasŭ ka?*	ee-ngheeree'soo noh gheenk*oh'*-sheehay' woh toh'ree-kah-eh'teh koo-dahs*i*mah's' kah?
A 10-yen Bank of Japan note	*Nippon Ginkō no jiu yen satsŭ*	neep'pohn gheenk*oh'* noh jew yen sah'ts'
A cheque	*Ko-gitte*	koh-ngheet'teh
A bill of exchange	*Kawase-tegata*	kahwah'seh teh-ngah'tah
Letter of credit	*Shinyō-jō*	sheen-*yoh'*-j*oh*
Banker's order	*Ginkō no shi-harai jō*	gheenkoh' noh shee-hah-ri' j*oh*
Money order (postal)	*Yūbin-kawase*	*yoo'*been-kahwah'seh
Telegraphic draft	*Denshin-kawase*	den'sheen-kahwah'seh

JAPANESE COINS.

[p.107.

MONEY, WEIGHTS & MEASURES.

(*Kingin; Kimme; Chō, tan, shaku.*)

NOTE.—With the exception of the *hiro* and the *tsubo*, all the names of the Measures, Weights, &c., given in the following tables are of Chinese origin, and are accompanied by the Chinese numerals only.

MONEY.

The currency is DECIMAL. The unit is the *yen*, a silver coin equivalent to about two English shillings (50 cents American), which has taken the place of the Mexican dollar, formerly used in Japan, but now obsolete.

One *yen* = 100 *sen*; one *sen* = 10 *rin*.

GOLD PIECES of 5, 10 and 20 *yen* are also coined.

COPPER COINS vary from one-tenth of a *sen* (1 *rin*) to 2 *sen*.

There is also a PAPER CURRENCY, consisting of notes of from 5 *sen* upwards. The smaller notes are most in use, such notes as 10 and 20 *yen* being used principally in commerce. Not only in towns, but throughout Japan generally, paper money, and especially that of the Bank of Japan, is regarded with more favour than gold or silver coin.

Banking transactions, and indeed commercial transactions in general, are framed on English models. Thus, ordinary and telegraphic money orders are issued; there is a Post Office Savings Bank; and Letters of Credit, Bills of Exchange and Bankers' Orders are all in constant use.

WEIGHT.

10 *rin*	=	1 *fun*	=	5.8 grs. (troy)
10 *fun*	=	1 *momme*	=	58 ,, ,,
100 *momme*	=	1 *hyaku-me*	=	about ¾ lb. (av.)
160 ,,	=	1 *kin**	=	1⅓ lb.
1000 ,,	=	1 *kwamme*	=	8.28 ,,

* Foreigners have mostly to do with ½ *kin*, 1 *kin* and upwards. 100 *kin* = 133⅓ lb. avoirdupois.

DRY GOODS MEASURE.

In measuring dry goods a *shaku* (termed *kujirajaku*) of 14.918 inches is employed. Silk and cotton goods are generally made up into pieces measuring a little more than 10¾ yards (*tan*) and also into pieces of double that length (*hiki*).

The English yard is now becoming generally known in towns

LONG MEASURE.

10 *rin*	= 1 *bu* ...	=	0.1193 in. (1/8 in.)
10 *bu*	= 1 *sun* ...	=	1.193 „ (1 1/5 in.)
10 *sun*	= {1 *shaku* or *kaneshaku*}	=	11.93 in. (nearly 1 foot)
6 *shaku*	= 1 *ken* ...	=	71.58 „ (nearly 2 yds.)
10 „	= 1 *jō* ...	=	119.3 „ (nearly 10 ft.)
60 *ken* (nearly)	= 1 *chō*	=	119.30 yds. (about 120 yds.)
36 *chō*	= 1 *ri* ...	=	2.44 miles

For nautical measurements, the *kai-ri*, which equals the European geographical mile, is now in general use; whilst for indicating the depth of water, the *hiro* (about 5 ft.) is employed.

SUPERFICIAL (LAND) MEASURE.

1 *tsubo*	= about 36 sq. ft.		
30 „	= 1 *se*	= 118.6 sq. yds.	
10 *se*	= 1 *tan*	= 1186 „	(over 1/4 acre)
10 *tan*	= 1 *chō*	= 2.45 acres (2 a. 1 r. 32 p.)	

The *tsubo* is the common unit of measurement.

MEASURE OF CAPACITY.

10 *sai*	= 1 *shaku*	=	1/31 pint
10 *shaku*	= 1 *gō*	=	about 1/3 pint
10 *gō*	= 1 *shō*	=	„ 3 1/5 pints
10 *shō*	= 1 *tō*	=	„ 4 gallons
10 *to*	= 1 *koku*	=	„ 39.7 „

This measure is employed for grain and liquids. The *shō* equals 0.397 (about two-fifths) of a gallon. The *koku* is employed for measuring junks, and is equal to about 4-27ths of a ton (nearly 3 cwt.), or 2 1/2 *piculs*. (1 *picul* = 100 *kin*.)

POSTAGE.

The postal rates *from* Japan to the United Kingdom are as follows:—

For Letters ...	10 sen for 20 grams.	6 sen additional 20 grams.
Postcards ...	6 sen	
Newspapers (ordinary)	2 sen	

To Japan, from the United Kingdom:—

Letters	2 1/2d. first oz. 1 1/2d. additional
Postcards ...	1 1/2d.
Newspapers ...	1/2d. for 2oz.

P.O.7.202.